MW00989315

BEHOLD THIS HEART

THOMAS F. DAILEY, O.S.F.S.

Behold This Heart

*ST. FRANCIS DE SALES AND
DEVOTION TO THE SACRED HEART*

SOPHIA INSTITUTE PRESS
Manchester, New Hampshire

Imprimi potest: Very Reverend Lewis Fiorelli, O.S.F.S.,
Provincial Superior, Oblates of St. Francis de Sales, June 30, 2020

Nihil obstat: Reverend Monsignor Joseph G. Prior,
Censor Librorum, Archdiocese of Philadelphia

Imprimatur: Most Reverend Nelson J. Pérez, D.D.,
Archbishop of Philadelphia, October 15, 2020

The *Nihil obstat* and *Imprimatur* are a declaration that a book or pamphlet is considered to be free from doctrinal or moral error. It is not implied that those who have granted the Nihil obstat and Imprimatur agree with the contents, opinions, or statements expressed.

Sophia Institute Press
Box 5284, Manchester, NH 03108
1-800-888-9344

www.SophiaInstitute.com

Sophia Institute Press® is a registered trademark of Sophia Institute.

Library of Congress Cataloging-in-Publication Data

Names: Dailey, Thomas F., author.

Title: Behold this heart : St. Francis de Sales and devotion to the sacred heart / Fr. Thomas F. Dailey, O.S.F.S..

Description: Manchester, NH : Sophia Institute Press, [2020] Includes bibliographical references. Summary: "Explains the Salesian devotion to the Sacred Heart of Jesus and includes a novena in that tradition"— Provided by publisher.

Identifiers: LCCN 2020035087 (print) LCCN 2020035088 (ebook) ISBN 9781644131336 ISBN 9781644131343 (ebook)

Subjects: LCSH: Sacred Heart, Devotion to. Francis, de Sales, Saint, 1567-1622.

Classification: LCC BX2157 .D35 2020 (print) LCC BX2157 (ebook) DDC 232— dc23

LC record available at https://lccn.loc.gov/2020035087

LC ebook record available at https://lccn.loc.gov/2020035088

First printing

To the Nuns in the Order of the
VISITATION OF HOLY MARY,
who, in the saintly tradition of

FRANCIS DE SALES,
JANE DE CHANTAL, and
MARGARET MARY ALACOQUE,

continue to behold the Sacred Heart of Jesus
and embody the love of God for the world
in their own loving hearts and praying hands.

CONTENTS

✠

Acknowledgments

Scripture quotations are from the ESV Catholic Edition with Deuterocanonical Books, published as *The Augustine Bible* by the Augustine Institute 2019 (ISBN 978-1-950939-09-1). Copyright © 2017 by Crossway, a publishing ministry of Good News Publishers. Used by permission. All rights reserved.

Unless otherwise noted, quotations from English translations of papal documents are from the Vatican website (w2.vatican.va) © Libreria Editrice Vaticana. All rights reserved. Used with permission.

Quotations from Francis de Sales, *Introduction to the Devout Life*, translated by Rt. Rev. John K. Ryan, copyright © 1950, 1952, 1966 by John K. Ryan, New York: Image Books, 1972/2003. Used with permission of Random House LLC.

Quotations from Francis de Sales, *Treatise on the Love of God*, 2 volumes, translated by Rt. Rev. John K. Ryan, copyright © 1963 by Doubleday & Company, Inc., copyright © 1974 by John K. Ryan, Rockford, IL: TAN Books and Publishers, 1975.

Quotations from *The Sermons of St. Francis de Sales on Our Lady*, edited by Father Lewis S. Fiorelli, O.S.F.S., translated by Nuns of the Visitation, copyright © 1985 by the Visitation Monastery of Frederick, MD, Inc., Rockford, IL: TAN Books and Publishers, 1985.

Behold This Heart

BEHOLD THIS HEART

Introduction

✠

"Behold this Heart, which has so loved men.
It is nothing but love and mercy!"

Here we find a simple invitation spoken by the Lord Jesus to St. Margaret Mary Alacoque in the late seventeenth century. Ever since, the invitation has resonated with men and women around the world.

The Lord invites devotees to a love story—not just a story *about* love, one that we listen to or learn from, but a story *of* love, a sacred tale that we best understand by entering into and participating in it.

In fact, "beholding" this Heart introduces us to a long-standing tradition of intertwining stories that prove to be both mind-boggling and life changing.

A Brief History of Devotion to the Sacred Heart

From the beginning of the Christian story, believers have taken a deep interest in the Heart of Jesus. That concern derives, specifically, from reflection on two passages in the Gospel of John: the scene at the Last Supper in which the beloved apostle reclines beside Jesus and rests his head on the Master's Heart (John 13:23–25), and the image of the pierced side of Jesus on the Cross from which blood and water flowed (John 19:34).

The early Church Fathers read those passages through an interpretive lens that allowed them to discover a spiritual meaning greater than that conveyed literally in the text. According to these patristic commentators, John's Gospel reveals the Sacred Heart of Jesus as the *fons vitae*, which Hugo Rahner describes as the "fountain of life [that] is the source of the church, of the gospels, of the sacraments, and of grace."[1]

In medieval times, that spiritual interpretation of the Gospel led monks and nuns to a more affective experience of union with Jesus through a contemplative focus on the physical hearts they share with Him. Some, such as St. Gertrude of Helfta (1256–1302) and St. Mechtilde of Hackeborn (1241–1298), even experienced a mystical "exchange of hearts" with the Savior.

Later in this period, Franciscan and Dominican friars spread devotion to the Sacred Heart by preaching and writing on the five wounds of the crucified Lord, the most prominent being His pierced side. They exhorted believers to find there the opening through which they could spiritually enter into union with Jesus and derive benefit from pondering the divine Heart wounded by love.

This contemplative focus on the suffering humanity of the Savior set the stage for St. Margaret Mary, whose personal experience

---

[1] Cited in Jeanne Weber, "Devotion to the Sacred Heart: History, Theology and Liturgical Celebration," *Worship* 72, no. 3 (1998): 238–239.

would prove to be life changing for so many. We can only wonder why the Lord chose to reveal His Sacred Heart to her with such depth, clarity, and intensity. Regardless, we know that from the mystical experience of this saintly nun—who lived a humble life, hidden away in a cloistered monastery in the bucolic countryside of eastern France—the cult of the Sacred Heart has developed into the universal devotion we know today.

Intriguing on its own, the story of St. Margaret Mary's visions of Jesus represents the zenith of the longer and larger story of Salesian spirituality. That tradition, characterized by a worldview of interconnected human and divine hearts,[2] owes its origins to St. Francis de Sales (1567–1622) and St. Jane Frances de Chantal (1572–1641). So close were their spiritual friendship and apostolic collaboration that these saints are described as having but "one heart and one soul."

Inspired by the biblical encounter between Mary and her cousin Elizabeth, Francis de Sales and Jane de Chantal jointly founded a new religious order—the Visitation of Holy Mary. The "base and foundation of their order," according to a letter of St. Jane, was that the Sisters would become "imitators of the two dearest virtues of the Sacred Heart of the incarnate Word, meekness and humility, which … would give them that particular privilege and that incomparable grace of bearing the quality of Daughters of the Heart of Jesus."[3]

---

[2] See Joseph Chorpenning, "*Lectio Divina* and Francis de Sales's Picturing of the Interconnection of Divine and Human Hearts," in *Imago Exegetica: Visual Images as Exegetical Instruments, 1400–1700*, eds. Walter S. Melion, James Clifton, and Michel Weemans (Leiden, Netherlands: Brill, 2014), 449–477.

[3] Cited in Henri L'Honoré, "Le culte du Coeur du Christ à la Visitation avant Marguerite-Marie," in *Sainte Marguerite-Marie et le message de*

Through that grace, in the Salesian way of prayer cultivated in the Visitation community at Paray-le-Monial, St. Margaret Mary would experience the Sacred Heart. From that monastery, through the apostolic fervor of St. Claude de la Colombière (1641–1682) and the missionary work of his fellow Jesuits,[4] the devotion would spread far and wide. And the school of spirituality in which this devotion was so central would go on to ignite a "Salesian Pentecost" in the nineteenth century and inspire the "universal call to holiness" at the Second Vatican Council in the mid-twentieth century.[5]

Since the Council, devotion to the Sacred Heart has figured prominently in papal teaching as it relates to the story of contemporary life:

* Pope St. John XXIII "considered devotion to the Sacred Heart as one of the three devotions on which the genuine Christian life is built," while Pope St. Paul VI "commended devotion to the Heart of Jesus above all 'as the most effective means of promoting the reform of life and the defeat of atheism.'" [6]

Paray-le-Monial, eds. Raymond Darricau and Bernard Peyrous (Paris: Desclée, 1993), 121.

[4] For more about the Jesuits' role in the spread of the devotion beyond Paray-le-Monial, see the texts of Pope St. John Paul II translated in the first appendix of this book.

[5] See Wendy Wright, *Heart Speaks to Heart: The Salesian Tradition*, Traditions of Christian Spirituality Series (Maryknoll, NY: Orbis Books, 2004).

[6] According to F. Schwendimann, as cited in Anton Mattes, "Devotion to the Heart of Jesus in Modern Times: The Influence of Saint Margaret Mary Alacoque," in *Faith in Christ and the Worship of Christ: New Approaches to Devotion to Christ*, ed. Leo Scheffczyk, trans. Graham Harrison (San Francisco: Ignatius Press, 1986), 110.

- Pope St. John Paul II claimed that in the new millennium, man "needs Christ's Heart to know God and to know himself; he needs it to build the civilization of love."[7]

- Pope Emeritus Benedict XVI adds that "when we practise this devotion, not only do we recognize God's love with gratitude but we continue to open ourselves to this love so that our lives are ever more closely patterned upon it.... This explains why the devotion, which is totally oriented to the love of God who sacrificed himself for us, has an irreplaceable importance for our faith and for our life in love."[8]

- Pope Francis has repeatedly referred to the Sacred Heart in terms of celebrating the "feast of love." In his meditations on this solemnity, he encourages us to realize that "when we seek him, he has sought us first: he is always before us, he waits to receive us in his heart, in his love."[9]

We do well to hand on the story of this devotion because, as Jeanne Weber concludes, "the symbol of the heart of Christ provides a point of entry into the entire paschal mystery," and it serves as "an enduring symbol which reveals the loving intimacy of a God who has in Christ transformed suffering and death

---

[7] "Letter of John Paul II on the 100th Anniversary of the Consecration of the Human Race to the Divine Heart of Jesus" (June 11, 1999), no. 1.

[8] "Letter of His Holiness Benedict XVI on the Occasion of the 50th Anniversary of the Encyclical *Haurietis Aquas*" (May 15, 2006).

[9] Pope Francis, "God's lullaby," Morning Meditation in the Chapel of the *Domus Sanctae Marthae* (June 27, 2014).

into life and who, through the power of the Spirit, does the same in us."[10]

Today, that symbol can be found piously displayed (or "enthroned") in many homes and churches. It also lies at the center of the worldwide cult of the Sacred Heart, a set of devotional practices including regular worship (through votive Masses and eucharistic adoration), personal acts of consecration, belief in the twelve promises made by the Lord to St. Margaret Mary, and even the formation of honor guards and other societies that promote this devotion. [11]

"Behold this Heart . . ."

The above invitation now draws us into the story of this book, the telling of which is inspired by the jubilee year (2019–2020) celebrating the centenary of the canonization of St. Margaret Mary Alacoque. As the superior of the monastery at Paray-le-Monial explains, the grace of that jubilee was conferred upon the monasteries of the Visitation of Holy Mary "so that the love of the Heart of Jesus might further shine forth over the world" and in the hope that it "could also allow the numerous faithful who frequent the chapels of [Visitation] monasteries to intimately experience the love of the Heart of Jesus, and to render him 'love for love' according to the desire that he himself had expressed to Saint Margaret Mary."[12]

---

[10] Weber, "Devotion to the Sacred Heart," 254.

[11] Examples of these practices can be found in the second appendix of this book.

[12] From the letter of Sr. Marie Simon Priou and the Sisters of Paray-le-Monial announcing the concession of the jubilee year, with the grace of a plenary indulgence, from the Apostolic Penitentiary (August 22, 2019).

This small work, based on more impressive studies by Wendy Wright and other scholars, seeks to kindle the "love for love" that enflames devotion to the Sacred Heart.

In part 1 we look more closely at the Salesian backstory to shed additional light on the key characters and spiritual vision that give shape to the sacred narrative. As we shall see, the theological worldview championed by St. Francis de Sales and St. Jane de Chantal serves as the remote source for this story, while the monastic life of the Visitation of Holy Mary provides its more proximate context. From within this Salesian tradition, St. Margaret Mary Alacoque emerges as the visionary promoter of the devotion, whose efficacy derives from the power of gazing contemplatively upon the image of the Sacred Heart of Jesus.

Part 2 considers the story of that sacred image inasmuch as it focuses our spiritual attention in Salesian prayer. As a distinctive avenue to understanding, meditation (or mental prayer) builds on the human faculty of visualization. That "imaginative" type of prayer, typical of monastic life, has been adapted by St. Francis de Sales for use by people seeking to live devout lives in the midst of worldly responsibilities. Following the saint's guidance, anyone and everyone can engage in meditative prayer to the Sacred Heart, in which seeing really is believing.

Then, in part 3, we tell the story anew through the structure of a spiritual novena. In nine successive chapters, we lead readers through a prayerful narration of the life of the Sacred Heart of Jesus. The genre of these "meditations" is more spiritual than systematic, their character more contemplative than conceptual. The makeup of this literary novena aims not to inform readers about historical and literary details of the biblical story (as would a commentary); rather, the novena seeks to inspire engagement with the central person in that story, by suggesting considerations for the mind, affections for the heart, and resolutions for the will—all in keeping with the Salesian approach to devotion.

In this way, we hope that those who take up this book will hear through its pages the same invitation to "behold this Heart which has so loved" the world—because the story of the Sacred Heart is ultimately the story of all our hearts, too, as we seek to discover the love of Jesus, which alone gives fulfillment to our restless longings in this life.[13]

[13] As Pope Francis notes in his Message for World Communications Day 2020: "The Bible is thus the great love story between God and humanity. At its centre stands Jesus, whose own story brings to fulfilment both God's love for us and our love for God. Henceforth, in every generation, men and women are called to recount and commit to memory the most significant episodes of this Story of stories, those that best communicate its meaning" (no. 3).

Part 1

The Salesian Backstory

✛

THE LIVING TRADITION OF A WORLD OF HEARTS

I n an image painted with words, Wendy Wright illustrates the
tradition of Salesian spirituality as envisioning and enabling *a
world of hearts*:

> Interconnected by their common natures, the divine heart
> and human hearts bridged by the human-divine heart of
> Jesus are the generative and vitalizing organs of a life which
> is at once spiritual and earthly. Together they breathe, they
> desire and they die. Together they form a reality, at once

vivid and creaturely, yet which opens wide onto the uncreated and limitless expanse of the divine.[14]

To contextualize this work of devotion, we first offer a brief "backstory" that considers the connections among St. Francis de Sales and St. Jane de Chantal; the Order of the Visitation of Holy Mary, which they co-founded; and St. Margaret Mary Alacoque, the Visitation nun to whom Jesus revealed His most Sacred Heart.

More-detailed biographies of these saints, histories of the Visitation Order, and studies of Salesian spirituality can be found elsewhere. Our purpose here is merely to draw from this abundant scholarship a few references that highlight the specific thoughts and personal experiences of each, as together they ground the living tradition of devotion to the Sacred Heart.

St. Francis de Sales (1567–1622) and St. Jane de Chantal (1572–1641)

Consistent with the humanism of his time and place, Francis de Sales, bishop of Geneva and Doctor of the Church, appropriated the notion that the heart is the living, undivided center of human life. Andre Brix explains the saint's thought as follows: "[Francis] means … that the 'heart,' which is the human being taken integrally, body and soul, in an indissociable

[14] Wendy Wright, "'That Is What It Is Made For': The Image of the Heart in the Spirituality of Francis de Sales and Jane de Chantal," in *Spiritualities of the Heart: Approaches to Personal Wholeness in Christian Tradition*, ed. Annice Callahan (Mahwah, NJ: Paulist Press, 1990), 154.

unity, is also the deepest 'me' and our mask, or better our 'person' who, by the heart, is known and recognized."[15]

Drawing on Aristotle's claim that the heart is the first organ to come to life and the last to die (*Treatise*, 11:7), Francis saw the heart as the central axis of human life, as that which distinguishes human beings from the rest of creation. Home to the passions (the emotional life), the heart is also where the more important decisions are made (with our free will) and what directs the brain toward meaningful action (the rational life).[16]

But as a *Christian* humanist, Francis recognized that the heart opens the way to so much more. For this holy teacher, the human heart serves as the principle and origin of the passions (*Treatise*, 6:13). It seeks to fulfill those passions by desiring something (or someone) that will bring us happiness. Yet, as we know, that search for meaning comes to no end in this life; because nothing of this world fully satisfies our deepest longings, we live a "restless" existence.

For Francis, however, that fundamental experience of human inquietude represented something positive. It led him to see the heart as the principle and origin of the spiritual life (*Treatise*, 1:10), because the natural inclination by which we desire and seek happiness points beyond ourselves. As he explains, this inclination opens us to a sense of the absolute that alone can bring meaning and fulfillment:

---

[15] Andre Brix, "Saint François de Sales et le 'Coeur,'" in Darricau and Peyrous, *Sainte Marguerite-Marie*, 66.

[16] References to primary Salesian sources (i.e., those authored by St. Francis de Sales or St. Jane de Chantal, or both) are cited in-text. Full information about each source is provided in the first section of the bibliography.

Now we have a natural inclination towards the supreme good, in consequence of which our heart has a certain inner anxiety and constant unrest, since it is able in no way either to calm itself or to cease to testify that it lacks perfect satisfaction and solid content.... It is thus by a deep and secret instinct that our heart tends in all its actions towards happiness and reaches out for happiness. It seeks it now here, now there, groping as it were without knowing where it abides or in what it consists until faith reveals it and describes its infinite marvels. Then, when it has found the treasure sought for, ah! what contentment comes to this poor human heart! What joy, what loving complacence! (*Treatise*, 2:15)

Thus, for Francis de Sales, the longings of the human heart lead toward God and our fulfillment in union with the divine Heart. This is what it means to be created by God and for God, in His "image and likeness." Union with divine love is the spiritual vocation of every human person, which the saint summarizes poetically in ascending terms when he writes: "Man is the perfection of the universe; the spirit is the perfection of man; love is that of the spirit; and Charity that of love. This is why love is the end, the perfection, and the excellence of the Universe" (*Treatise*, 10:1).

In light of this excellence for which we have been created, Francis de Sales sees in the human heart a sacred space, a place opened up for us in and through the gift of God's love. In that space we feel an affinity for God. There we find a congruence between human need and divine abundance, between the human capacity to receive and the divine nature to give. There our natural desire for happiness can be met by the "God of the human heart" whose supernatural grace fulfills us:

As soon as a man gives a little attentive thought to the divinity he feels a certain sweet emotion within his heart, and this testifies that God is God of the human heart. Our mind is never so filled with pleasure as during such thoughts of the divinity.... This pleasure, this confidence that man's heart naturally has in God, assuredly comes from nowhere but the congruity existing between God's goodness and our soul. It is a great but secret congruity; a congruity that all men know but few understand, a congruity that can neither be denied nor easily penetrated. We are created to the image and likeness of God. What does this mean if not that we have the utmost congruity with his divine majesty? (*Treatise*, 1:15)

But we cannot achieve this happy end on our own. Our imperfection impedes us along the way. Owing to the ravages of Original Sin, compounded by our actual sins, human knowledge is confused and the will weakened. To make our lives eternally meaningful, a Savior is needed.

Thus, says Francis, only in the Heart of the Redeemer, in the fully divine and fully human Heart of Jesus, is love perfected (*Treatise*, 6:12). Christ's Resurrection proves this. Our faith assures us of it, for "faith makes us know with infallible certitude that God exists, that he is infinite in goodness, that he can communicate himself to us, and that not only can he do so but he will do so. Hence with ineffable sweetness he has prepared for us all the means necessary to attain to the happiness of immortal glory" (*Treatise*, 2:15). With that faith, we can hope in what otherwise seems futile, and we are able to love as well as we can.

Thus, in Salesian spirituality, cultivating Christian faith through asceticism and devotion is primarily a matter of the heart. These spiritual practices develop the interior life, which, in turn, shapes the exterior life. As the saint famously writes in his classic work on devotion:

> Since the heart is the source of our actions, as the heart is so are they.... In short, whoever wins a man's heart has won the whole man. Yet even the heart, where we wish to begin, must be instructed as to how it should model its outward conduct and bearing so that by them men can see not only holy devotion but also great wisdom and prudence. (*Introduction*, 3:23)

The Christian, then, learns to live a life of virtue (effective love) by first attending to the prayer of his or her heart (affective love). The desire that begins in the heart leads to the happiness we seek when we let our hearts "breathe" with God. In the mutual, organic movement of the heart, we breathe in the inspirations of God's grace and breathe out the aspirations of our thoughts and words and deeds. When our heart beats and breathes in union with God's, our respirations fill us with new life as we move toward the goal of being interconnected in love—with our neighbor in this life and with God eternally.

No one understood this spirituality of the heart better than Jane Frances de Chantal. Wife, mother, estate manager, and community philanthropist, Jane knew from personal experience the varied workings of the human heart. But her heart and her entire life would change dramatically when her husband was killed in a hunting accident. Then, in 1604, she had an inspired encounter that would prove pivotal in her own life and instrumental in fostering subsequent devotion to the Sacred Heart. As Wright summarizes it, Jane

> had come to the Lenten sermons in Dijon, the city of her birth, at the invitation of her father Bénigne Frémyot, a magistrate in the local parliament.... The popular sermon series was to be preached by the charismatic bishop from Savoy. When Francis de Sales stepped out into the pulpit that March of 1604, an astonished Jane recognized him as the man wo had recently appeared to her in a strange vision as, in her grief, she had been riding on her baronial estates.[17]

Soon afterward, she would become the most beloved spiritual daughter of Francis de Sales.

But Jane was not merely the prime recipient of Francis's spiritual wisdom. Her life, according to Hélène Bordes, served as a living laboratory in which this emerging spiritual tradition would become incarnate and brought to life.[18] Through the spiritual intimacy of a lifelong friendship and collaborative apostolate—their "bond of perfection"—Jane joined with Francis to give birth to the Salesian tradition of a world of hearts.[19] As Wright describes it, their relationship "expressed their belief in the spiritual reality

---

[17] Wright, *Heart Speaks to Heart*, 44-45.

[18] Hélène Bordes, "La méditation du mystère de la Visitation par François de Sales et l'esprit de l'Ordre de la Visitation," in *Visitation et Visitandines aux XVIIe et XVIIIe siècles*, Actes de Colloque d'Annecy, 1999, eds. Bernard Dompnier and Dominique Julia (Saint-Étienne, France: Publications de l'Université de Saint-Étienne, 2001), 69-70.

[19] See Wendy Wright, *Bond of Perfection: Jeanne de Chantal and François de Sales* (Mahwah, NJ: Paulist Press, 1983).

of hearts aflame with the love of God leading other hearts more deeply into the divine embrace."[20] And that union of hearts would come to fruition through the relational mystery of the new religious community that these two saints jointly founded and in which devotion to the Sacred Heart would be engendered.[21]

The Visitation of Holy Mary

The formation of a religious community inspired by the biblical mystery of Mary's visit to Elizabeth would realize, in an innovative way, the trajectory of the heart that Francis de Sales elaborated upon as the vocation of all persons. Specifically, it would engage those devout women who, owing to circumstances of age or ability or other duties, would not otherwise be suited to contemplative life in a monastery as it was then practiced. As the religious historian Elisabeth Stopp notes:

> An uncloistered community, doing a small amount of active work outside, open to older women and widows as well as to the ordinary young postulant, receiving those who longed for the contemplative state of life although their health might not be sufficiently robust to stand the hardship of a more austere rule, substituting the simpler Little Office of Our Lady for the full office—all this meant real innovation at the beginning of the seventeenth century.[22]

---

[20] Wright, *Heart Speaks to Heart*, 48.

[21] See Wendy Wright, "Margaret Mary Alacoque and the Relational Mystery of the Visitation of Holy Mary," *Theological Review of the Episcopal Academy* (Spring 2006).

[22] Elisabeth Stopp, *Hidden in God: Essays and Talks on St. Jane Frances de Chantal*, ed. Terence O'Reilly (Philadelphia: St. Joseph's University Press, 1999), 17.

Consistent with the Salesian understanding of the spiritual life as primarily a matter of the heart, Jane de Chantal and three other ladies in Annecy (the French town in which the bishop of Geneva resided) began this new initiative on June 6, 1610. They would take for their little group the name of "The Visitation of Holy Mary" in recognition of the biblical mystery which, for the two co-founders, narratively summarized Christianity in a tale of human hearts inspired by the Spirit of Love. As Wright explains:

> The kingdom of God, the reign of divine love, is thus in Salesian spirituality aptly imaged as a visitation—a union of divine and human love, a love most vividly realised on earth as spiritual friendship. The reciprocity of the love of friends, that shared and mutually transforming relationship, is the model of the kingdom come.[23]

That relational model characterized the life of the Visitation, a simplified religious order whose sole aim was to embody the loving virtues of humility toward God and gentleness toward neighbor. Their "hidden" life together was to find its source and succor in the Sacred Heart, as we learn from Bougaud's biography of St. Margaret Mary.[24] We see this emphasis in the recommendations given by Francis to Jane and the other Sisters at the start of this new initiative:

> At the moment of Mme. de Chantal's departure for Annecy to begin the foundation of the Institute, St. Francis de Sales wrote her a line to animate her courage: "My advice, my

---

[23] Wright, *Heart Speaks to Heart*, 53.

[24] Émile Bougaud, *The Life of St. Margaret Mary Alacoque*, trans. a Visitandine of Baltimore (Rockford, IL: TAN Books and Publishers, 1990). Hereafter cited in text as *Life*.

daughter, is, that henceforth we live no more in ourselves, but that in heart, intention, and confidence *we lodge forever in the pierced side of the Savior*."

Again, on the eve of her entrance: "My daughter, I must tell you that I have never seen so clearly how much you are my daughter as now. But I say it as I see it in the Heart of our Saviour. O my daughter, how I desire that your life be hidden with Jesus Christ in God! I am going to make a little prayer for this, in which I shall implore the royal heart of the Saviour for ours."

And to his daughters gathered around him in those first sweet moments of the little "Gallery House," he says: "The other day, considering in prayer the open side of the Saviour, and gazing upon *His Heart*, I seemed to see all our hearts around His, doing Him homage as the Sovereign King of hearts." (*Life*, 145–146)

We see this same focus in Jane's counsel: "If the Sisters of the Visitation are very humble and faithful to God, they shall have the Heart of Jesus for a dwelling and sojourn in this world" (*Life*, 146). She expresses this conviction even more clearly in a meditation she commended to her Sisters on the basis of Francis's writings:

Consider that the sweet Saviour not only showed His love for us, as well as for all other Christians, by the work of our redemption; but that He obliges us especially, as daughters of the Visitation, by the gift and favor that He has made to our Order and to each of us in particular of His Heart, or rather of the virtues it contains, since He has founded our most lovely Institute on these two precepts: Learn of Me that I am meek and humble of heart. This is the portion of His treasures that has fallen to us. Having given to other Orders, to one eminent prayer, to another solitude, to another austerity, He bequeathed to us what, undoubtedly, He esteemed more dear, since His precious Heart is its depository. Ah, could we but have this satisfaction, could we learn and practise well the lesson that this loving Savior gives us, we should then be honored in bearing the title of 'Daughters of the Heart of Jesus'." (*Life*, 153–154)

Beyond the verbal explanations given by the saintly founders, the interconnection between the hearts of the Visitandines and the Sacred Heart soon came to be graphically depicted in the coat of arms chosen for this new religious community. A year after establishing the new community, on what turned out later to be the very day on which the Lord requested that the solemnity of the Sacred Heart be celebrated (the Friday after the octave of Corpus Christi), Francis wrote a letter to Jane in which he disclosed a thought given him by God, namely

> that our house of the Visitation is by his grace, noble and important enough to have its own coat of arms, its escutcheon, its device, and its battle cry. So I have thought, dear Mother, if you agree, we should take as our coat of arms a single heart pierced by two arrows, the whole enclosed in a crown of thorns, and with the poor heart serving to hold and support a cross which is to surmount it; and the heart is to be engraved with the sacred names of Jesus and Mary. (*Selected Letters*, 193)

Yet the strongest connection in this Salesian world of hearts, one that surpasses the co-founders' advice and the institute's graphic identity, ultimately emerges from the characteristic style of prayer in a Visitation monastery. According to Hélène Bordes and Jean-Marie Lemaire, "the grand characteristic of Salesian mysticism and therefore of Visitandine prayer [is] the voluntary and persevering movement of God toward man and of man toward God."[25] That encounter happens in the heart. For the Sisters of the Visitation, it is experienced through the "simplicity" of prayer, described in terms of a union with the divine that comes from being in God's presence, from regarding the God who is present, or from abandoning oneself entirely to the divine will and providential care with which God remains present. And the privileged place for this encounter of hearts lies in the wounds of Christ, in His Heart, on the Cross.

Francis de Sales understood the power of that prayerful encounter and taught it as a form of mysticism of the heart. Through her shared encounters with Francis in spiritual direction, Jane de Chantal experienced an encounter of hearts and modeled a persevering union with the divine Heart. From these co-founders, the Visitation of Holy Mary learned of this encounter and strove to embrace and embody it by way of a continual abandonment to the Heart of Jesus.

In the context of this saintly tradition, through moments of prayer in a Visitation monastery at Paray-le-Monial, the nun with whom Salesian devotion to the Sacred Heart is most closely associated would experience the greatest of mystical encounters.

---

[25] Hélène Bordes and Jean-Marie Lemaire, "L'oraison Visitandine et les sources de Marguerite-Marie," in Darricau and Peyrous, *Sainte Marguerite-Marie*, 81.

St. Margaret Mary Alacoque (1647–1690)

From a young age, St. Margaret Mary seems to have known the trajectory of her life. On the one hand, she experienced much suffering; yet wishing neither to avoid nor to escape her pain, she aspired to share it with her crucified Lord as a means of cultivating a pure love for God. On the other hand, she ardently sought a contemplative life in which she could be consumed with prayer in His presence. These complementary desires would coalesce to form the way of abandonment to the Sacred Heart of Jesus soon after she entered the Visitation monastery on June 12, 1671.

Her aspiration to share in the Lord's Passion qualified the whole of St. Margaret Mary's existence and became the interpretive key to what she would experience in the revelation of the Sacred Heart. In concert with Jean-Claude Sagne's analysis of the saint's spiritual personality, Wright claims that "in imitation of Jesus, whose interior suffering was the deep secret of his heart, Margaret Mary's entire life is reviewed through the lens of interior suffering, a suffering mirroring the obedient love that the Son had for the Father. Her road ... was the road of abandonment of self in loving participation with the heart of Jesus, who so abandoned himself in passionate love."[26]

Wright further explains that this spiritual sense was characteristic of the religious culture of her time, for "the hallmark of the French or Bérullian school of spirituality which dominated the ethos of the grand siècle's second half was an emphasis on the

---

[26] Wright, "Relational Mystery of the Visitation," 5.

grandeur and omnipotence of God alongside a corresponding emphasis on human nothingness or *anéantissement*."[27] Yet this spirituality almost prevented the world from learning about the foundation of the devotion to the Sacred Heart, for Margaret Mary would speak of her experience with resistance and only as an act of obedience to her spiritual director.[28]

That experience consisted of three apparitions that the Lord made to her in which He revealed His Sacred Heart. These visionary experiences took place over the course of two years, beginning when she was but twenty-six years old and professed as a nun for only two years. In her autobiography, a quasi-diary of her lifelong dialogue with the Divinity, Margaret Mary wrote openly about numerous communications she had from God, both visual and auditory. Yet the three encounters between 1673 and 1675 stand out even more vividly for what was made known to her and for what was requested of her.

The first apparition occurred on December 27, 1673—the feast of St. John the Apostle, the same beloved disciple who reclined his head on the Master's chest at the Last Supper. According to Margaret Mary's account:

> Once, being before the Blessed Sacrament and having a little more leisure than usual, I felt wholly filled with this Divine Presence, and so powerfully moved by it that I forgot myself and the place in which I was. I abandoned myself to this Divine Spirit, and yielded my heart to the power of

---

[27] Wright, "Relational Mystery of the Visitation," 11–12.

[28] *The Autobiography of St. Margaret Mary Alacoque*, translation of the authentic French text by the Sisters of the Visitation in Partridge Green, Horsham, West Sussex (Rockford, IL: TAN Books and Publishers, 1986), 19.

His love. He made me rest for a long time on His divine breast, where He discovered to me the wonders of His love and the inexplicable secrets of His Sacred Heart, which *He had hitherto kept hidden from me. Now He opened it to me for the first time,* but in a way so real, so sensible, that it left me no room to doubt, though I am always in dread of deceiving myself. (*Life,* 163–164)

In this divine disclosure, the Lord revealed His plan for a new and greater devotion. The saint recounts what He said to her:

My Divine Heart is so passionately in love with men that it can no longer contain within itself the flames of its ardent charity. It must pour them out by thy means, and manifest itself to them to enrich them with its precious treasures, which contain all the graces of which they have need to be saved from perdition.... I have chosen thee as an abyss of unworthiness and ignorance to accomplish so great a design, so that all may be done by Me. (*Life,* 164)

Then, as confirmation of and empowerment for this call, the saint experienced a mystical "exchange of hearts" with her Savior. In her words,

He demanded my heart, and I supplicated Him to take it. He did so, and put it into His own Adorable Heart, in which He allowed me to see it as a little atom being consumed in that fiery furnace. Then, drawing it out like a burning flame in the form of a heart, He put it into the place whence He had taken it, saying: "Behold, My beloved, a precious proof of My love. I enclose in thy heart a little spark of the most ardent flame of My love, to serve thee as a heart and to consume thee till thy last moment." He

added: "Until now thou hast taken only the name of My
slave; henceforth thou shalt be called the well-beloved disciple of My Sacred Heart." (*Life*, 165)

Thus began the Sacred Heart devotion, within St. Margaret
Mary personally. Like the experience of other female visionaries,
St. Margaret Mary's "exchange of hearts" points to a transformation
at the core of her being, which Wright explains as "an experience
of radical experiential participation in the Christ event as it is
focused on the heart of the crucified and the experience of loving
conformity to or union with his suffering life."[29] First focused
on Margaret Mary alone, the devotion would take a step toward
expansion to all the faithful with the next apparition.

Though the exact date is unknown, most believe the second
apparition to have taken place six months after the first, in June
of 1674. As the saint recounts:

Once when the Blessed Sacrament was exposed, my
soul being absorbed in extraordinary recollection, Jesus
Christ, my sweet Master, presented Himself to me. He
was brilliant with glory; His five wounds shone like five
suns. Flames darted forth from all parts of His sacred
humanity, but especially from His adorable breast, which
resembled a furnace, and which, opening, displayed to me
His loving and amiable Heart, the living source of these
flames. (*Life*, 168)

[29] Wendy Wright, "Inside My Body Is the Body of God: Margaret
Mary Alacoque and the Tradition of Embodied Mysticism," in
*The Mystical Gesture: Essays on Medieval and Early Modern Spiritual
Culture in Honor of Mary E. Giles*, ed. Robert Boenig (Aldershot,
UK: Ashgate, 2000), 189.

Then, as in the first apparition, the Lord spoke to her, though this time in a more plaintive tone. As she recounts it:

> He unfolded to me … the inexplicable wonders of His pure love, and to what an excess He had carried it for the love of men, from whom He had received only ingratitude. "This is," He said, "much more painful to Me than all I suffered in My Passion. If men rendered Me some return of love, I should esteem little all I have done for them, and should wish, if such could be, to suffer it over again; but they meet My eager love with coldness and rebuffs. Do you, at least," said He in conclusion, "console and rejoice Me, by supplying as much as you can for their ingratitude." (*Life*, 168–169)

Immediately after, the Lord made known to her two things she was to do in response to this revelation: first, to receive Holy Communion on the first Friday of every month, and second, to spend an hour in prayer the night before. While these practices would later become important elements of devotion to the Sacred Heart, at the time, they were merely personal exercises, which this holy nun practiced for the sake of making amends for the ingratitude with which the Sacred Heart had been received by all men and women. That individual initiative would be broadened with the next apparition.

A year later—on June 16, 1675, the Friday following the octave of Corpus Christi—the final apparition took place. Once again, while Margaret Mary was at prayer before the tabernacle, the Lord appeared on the altar and revealed His Heart, saying:

> Behold … this heart which has so loved men that it has spared nothing, even to exhausting and consuming itself, in

order to testify its love. In return, I receive from the greater part only ingratitude, by their irreverence and sacrilege, and by the coldness and contempt they have for Me in this sacrament of love.

Then came the great request and corresponding promise that would lead to the devotion as we now know it:

> It is for this reason I ask thee that the first Friday after the octave of the Blessed Sacrament be appropriated to a special feast, to honor My Heart by communicating on that day, and making reparation for the indignity that it has received. And I promise that My Heart shall dilate to pour out abundantly the influences of its love on all that will render it this honor or procure its being rendered. (*Life*, 176)

And with that, the great apparitions of the Sacred Heart to St. Margaret Mary came to an end. A worldwide devotion, born of her mystical experience, would soon begin to emerge. As Bougaud concludes, "That which in silence and ecstasy she had three times consecutively beheld in that chapel, through that grate, on that altar, the Church also was going to see" (*Life*, 178).

By today's standards, Margaret Mary's supernatural experiences may seem odd, if not outright bizarre. However, in keeping with the theology of the Incarnation—in which God took on flesh and became human—St. Margaret Mary's visions can make sense when considered relative to the contemplative tradition of "embodied mysticism." She truly experienced the presence of Jesus directly before her. She mystically exchanged hearts with Him. She became so vividly conscious of Him, and of participating intimately in the redemption wrought by His Sacred

Heart, that she was physically and spiritually transformed by her experience.[30]

Still, even though Margaret Mary dutifully disclosed these apparitions to her religious superiors, they were not immediately accepted; cold, in fact, was the reception given to the lowly, timid nun by others in the same monastery.[31] After all, the admittedly ecstatic character of these moments in the prayer of such a young religious did not gel with the simple, hidden spirituality of her religious order, as Wright explains:

> Novel devotions and extraordinary spiritual experiences were suspect, both in the Visitation and in the general spiritual climate of the time. At the end of the seventeenth century, Visitandine life was idealized as simple and humble obedience to the community rule; sisters were lauded to the extent that they could be seen as "living rules." The young professed visionary, always somewhat unique, was scrutinized, and her humility was tested in many ways.[32]

Nevertheless, we can see in them, as did those who would investigate and confirm the saint's account, a progressive spiritual realization consistent with an experience of divine revelation. The origin of this revelation is the bountiful love of God for His people. That love, which by nature moves beyond itself for the sake of others, made itself known first to one (Margaret Mary) and then to many. Moving beyond personal faith and devotion, it enters into public view, into liturgical worship centered on the Most Blessed

---

[30] Wright, "Inside My Body Is the Body of God," 192.

[31] Marilyn Masse, "La Visitation et la devotion au Sacré-Coeur," in Dompnier and Julia, *Visitation et Visitandines*, 454.

[32] Wright, *Heart Speaks to Heart*, 100–101.

Sacrament. Notwithstanding the tepid response to this Real Presence from sinful human beings, divine love continues to pour itself out to the world, its streams flowing eventually into what would become a universal celebration of spiritual consolation.

The subsequent story of how the three revelations of the Sacred Heart to St. Margaret Mary would become a worldwide devotion presents a remarkable and fascinating tale of divine grace and human endeavor. Critical factors along the way include

- the supportive work of Claude de la Colombière (1641–1682), the Jesuit confessor at Paray-le-Monial who confirmed for Margaret Mary the veracity of her experiences and who consecrated himself, as she did, to making this revelation known;
- the assignment of St. Margaret Mary as novice mistress, which allowed her to teach the next generation of Visitandines to celebrate the Sacred Heart with special devotion;
- the correspondence St. Margaret Mary shared with others in Visitation monasteries, through whom devotion to the Sacred Heart would find its first home in the "souls and spaces" of the Sisters and of the monastery chapels;[33]
- the apostolic work of the Society of Jesus, and in particular the studies by Jean Croiset (1656–1738) and Joseph de Gallifet (1663–1749), which gave theological approbation to the saintly life and mission of Margaret Mary;[34]
- the network of Visitation monasteries near the "epicenter" of Paray-le-Monial—especially in Dijon, Moulins,

[33] Masse, "La Visitation," 467–472.
[34] Wright, *Heart Speaks to Heart*, 104.

and Nantes—whose superiors relayed the message of Margaret Mary;[35]

* the steadfastness of other Visitation monasteries in France—such as those at Auxerre, Mâcon, Caen, and Bourg—whose devotion to the Sacred Heart later enabled them to withstand the spreading influence of Jansenism and the eventual storm of the French revolution (*Life*, 362–370);

* the establishment of confraternities of lay people, beginning in 1825, whose free association as the "Guard of Honor" for the Sacred Heart reflected its popularity among the masses beyond the monastery and diffused the devotion into the lives of the local churches;[36]

* the approbation of the Church, through the establishment of the universal feast day of the Sacred Heart by Pope Pius IX in 1856 and its subsequent upgrade in liturgical rank in 1899 by Pope Leo XIII, who also consecrated the Church and the entire human race to the Sacred Heart;[37]

* the pioneering work of Fr. Matthew Crawley-Boevey and his followers, beginning in 1907, who promoted the "enthronement" of the Sacred Heart in homes, schools, hospitals, and even prisons throughout the world (*Life*, 378–380);

* the construction of churches specifically dedicated to the Sacred Heart, including the monumental basilica at

[35] Masse, "La Visitation," 472–478.

[36] Masse, "La Visitation," 478–481.

[37] Mattes, "Devotion to the Heart of Jesus in Modern Times," 108–110.

Montmartre in Paris whose consecration was proclaimed in 1914;

* and, finally, the canonization of St. Margaret Mary on May 13, 1920, after a lengthy and particularly severe and complex process, by which she "is situated perfectly ... as witness to a spirituality that encompasses every existence and enriches the person penetrated by the grace of God."[38]

The centuries-long development of this devotion began with two saints' view of life as one in which human and divine hearts are interconnected. It reached its zenith in extraordinary apparitions to an ordinary nun "hidden" in a Visitation monastery who would herself be canonized. It thrives in our day through the now universal celebration of the Sacred Heart of Jesus. The appeal of this devotion, as we shall explore in part 2, continues to be driven by a prayerful attentiveness to the image of the Sacred Heart as it was revealed to St. Margaret Mary Alacoque.

---

[38] Bernard Ardura, "Les procès de béatification et de canonisation de sainte Marguerite-Marie," in Darricau and Peyrous, Sainte Marguerite-Marie, 496.

Part 2

Salesian Prayer

CULTIVATING AN INSPIRED VISION

Born of St. Margaret Mary's vision, the widespread practice of devotion to the Sacred Heart owes a great deal to the power of images. In the "visualist paradigm" that this devotion embraces, multiple images of the Sacred Heart engender ideas, express meanings, excite passions, and invite reflections. The evolution of this iconography shows the power of the religious imagination at work. In the Salesian tradition, the imagination plays a key role in cultivating the "mystique" of the Sacred Heart of Jesus by informing how people pray. Following the methodology of meditation (or mental prayer) taught by St. Francis de Sales, what is familiar to contemplative nuns in a Visitation monastery—namely, an experience of the union of human and divine hearts—also becomes possible for those who lead active lives in the world.

The Visualist Paradigm of the Sacred Heart

Art has long depicted the sacred. In the Christian tradition, images of the faith abound, appearing in paintings, sculptures, icons, and stained-glass windows, not to mention architecture, literature, music, and other media. But the inspirational power of religious imagery extends beyond the material quality of the construct to encompass, express, and engage a spiritual dimension at work in the one who truly "sees" the images for what they are.

The Religious Imagination

The various images of the Sacred Heart exhibit that spiritual power. Whatever the medium in which the sacred image is depicted, it draws us into the mystery of God's sacrificial love for human beings. Gazing upon the Sacred Heart in prayer transports the viewer into the vital center of Jesus Himself.

The singularly distinctive feature of the Sacred Heart devotion, according to David Morgan, is its "visualist paradigm." Focusing on the image that points to the reality of the crucified Christ draws us into an experience that links story and memory, feeling and emotion, history and liturgy. Referring specifically to St. Margaret Mary, Morgan points to the visual vitality of her spiritual life; for her, "pictures became the means of imagination, serving as the medium for visionary experience, and visionary experience issued in the endorsement of imagery as productive of piety and devotion."[39]

As Morgan further explains, images like the Sacred Heart have a unique power to touch people in a way that goes beyond making sense. "Images are not inanimate signifiers," he writes, "but active

[39] David Morgan, "The Visual Piety of the Sacred Heart," *Material Religion* 13, no. 2 (2017): 235.

agents that shape and structure the experience of saints, self, and the divine."[40]

In this sense, a sacred image is not something just to look at. It is meant to be seen. The difference calls forth a uniquely human power of perception. When we truly "see" a sacred image, we not only look at it; we are acted upon by it. In a certain sense, the image looks back at us, does something to us, and challenges us to be something more. Really seeing it invites us to become what we perceive, to participate in what is depicted there, even to emulate what the image represents.

Similarly, Wendy Wright describes this paradigm in terms of a "primal image" and a "focal symbol."[41] The former expresses in a non-discursive way the very mystery that gives meaning and shape to the Christian life. The latter zeroes in on what is symbolized in that image as a standard for Christian identity.

As Wright further explains, religious images like the Sacred Heart possess a twofold, reciprocal power. On the one hand, they aid our understanding by helping us to "see" life differently. Sacred images enable us to imagine a new world, not in the sense of fiction or fantasy, but as a matter of possibility, reflecting the new way of life inaugurated in the saving words and deeds of Jesus. On the other hand, sacred images inspire us to become what we see, to be what we imagine, by living the truths that the image represents. Engaging the whole person—by exciting our emotions, informing our intellects, and vivifying our desires—sacred images shape us to dwell in that new world and live that new way of life.[42]

[40] Morgan, "Visual Piety," 233.

[41] See Wendy Wright, "A Wide and Fleshy Love: Images, Imagination, and the Heart of God," *Studies in Spirituality* 10 (2000): 255-274.

[42] Wright, "A Wide and Fleshy Love," 264-265.

Behold This Heart

Images of the Sacred Heart

The power of religious images to structure our view of the world and to form how we live in it may explain the long-standing appeal of the Sacred Heart and the fervent devotion to it. From visions to sketches, paintings to pictures, small emblems to grand statues—the evolution of the imagery associated with the Sacred Heart of Jesus shows its power to connect with viewers intimately and powerfully, so much so that the image and the devotion remain intertwined.[43]

The image of the Sacred Heart of Jesus clearly animated the vision of St. Francis de Sales and St. Jane de Chantal. It underlay their view of the world as made up of interconnected hearts. It informed their conception of their new religious order, as we see in the Visitandine coat of arms. Wright explains this further:

Visitandine spirituality in fact was a spirituality of human and divine hearts. It focused on an inner transformation so that Jesus could "live" in the heart through the acquisition of the virtues of the One who was "gentle and humble of heart." The cross and coat of arms of the Visitation community bore representations of the heart of the wounded savior that mirrored popular devotional images widely circulated at the time. And the sisters were recorded as considering themselves "imitators of the

---

[43] See David Morgan, *The Sacred Heart of Jesus: The Visual Evolution of a Devotion* (Amsterdam: Amsterdam University Press, 2008).

virtues of the Sacred Heart," as "made by and for the Sacred Heart," or as "daughters of the Heart of Jesus."[44]

To make the spiritual focus clear, upon the first profession of their religious vows, the Sisters receive a cross engraved on both sides. By their wearing it, St. Francis de Sales wrote, "everybody will know that our daughters belong to Jesus Christ crucified."[45]

Wearing that same profession cross, St. Margaret Mary would advance the iconography of the Sacred Heart in the latter part of the seventeenth century based on her memory of the apparitions. For her own veneration, she sketched an image that, at its core, included the wounded Heart, the holy Cross, and the crown of thorns. As she explained in one of her letters:

> I saw this divine Heart as on a throne of flames, more brilliant than the sun and transparent as crystal. It had Its adorable wound and was encircled with a crown of thorns, which signified the pricks our sins caused Him. It

---

[44] Wright, "A Wide and Fleshy Love," 259.

[45] Margaret Mary, "Visitation Nun's Profession Cross," "*Ask for Nothing, Refuse Nothing*" (blog), November 18, 2011, http://visitationdepository ofsacredheart.blogspot.com/2011/11/vistation-nuns-profession-cross.html. This source includes an explanation of the symbols on the profession cross.

was surmounted by a cross which signified that, from the first moment of His Incarnation, that is, from the time this Sacred Heart was formed, the cross was planted in It; that It was filled, from the very first moment, with all the bitterness, humiliations, poverty, sorrow, and contempt His sacred humanity would have to suffer during the whole course of His life and during His holy Passion.[46]

Functioning as an "ideogram,"[47] the sketch was shared with other Visitation monasteries to enhance the personal piety of the Sisters, as the original had done for the saint. When placed upon altars, near crucifixes, or in dedicated chapels, the emblematic image inspired a contemplative gazing upon the Sacred Heart that would become a hallmark of the devotion. As St. Margaret Mary writes, the Heart of God "must be honored under the symbol of this Heart of Flesh, Whose image He wished to be publicly exposed.... Wherever this sacred image would be exposed for veneration He would pour forth His graces and blessings."[48]

A new moment in the picturing of the Sacred Heart came with a shift from homemade sketches to anatomical images. The more

---

[46] *The Letters of St. Margaret Mary Alacoque,* trans. Clarence A. Herbst, S.J. (Rockford, IL: TAN Books and Publishers, 1997), 229. On June 20, 1686, St. Margaret Mary and her novices venerated this image for the first time on a small altar in the monastery at Paray-le-Monial.

[47] "The highly emblematic image registers the meaning of the Sacred Heart through symbolic motifs rather than literally portraying the heart as a human organ, as later depictions would do so carefully." David Morgan, "Rhetoric of the Heart: Figuring the Body in Devotion to the Sacred Heart," in *Things: Religion and the Question of Materiality,* eds. Dick Houtman and Birgit Meyer (New York: Fordham University Press, 2012), 93.

[48] *Letters of St. Margaret Mary Alacoque,* 230.

visceral image of the Heart of flesh, consistent with the intensity of feeling in Baroque spirituality, gave emphasis to the notion of reparation prominent in the saint's mystical apparitions. As Morgan explains:

> Human suffering's embodied nature was met and affirmed in the dissected viscera of Jesus. Reparations were powerfully repaid through devotion to the Heart, and the issuing of indulgences by bishops and popes, beginning as early as 1692, just two years after Alacoque's death, assured the currency of the devotion in the spiritual economy of compensating God for the debt of sin.[49]

As worship of the Sacred Heart developed following papal recognition of the feast, new imagery emphasized the Heart in closer relation to the Person of Jesus. In what may be the most prominent of all paintings of the Sacred Heart, Pompeo Batoni presents Christ holding His own Heart. What is new in this fuller rendering of the Savior, according to Morgan, "is the penetrating gaze of the figure, now understood as a portrait that seeks out the viewer's eye for an intimate connection, as if the image pleads for a personal and thoroughgoing response from those who look at it."[50]

Later still, during the French Revolution, the image of the Sacred Heart was appropriated as an insignia, the wearing of which carried political overtones. In the century that followed, the Heart of Jesus, heretofore depicted by itself or as separated from His body, appeared in images that placed the organ back

[49] Morgan, *Sacred Heart of Jesus*, 14.

[50] Morgan, *Sacred Heart of Jesus*, 16.

within the chest of the Savior, whose tunic was opened to reveal it or whose hand pointed to it. This, says Morgan, "changed the way that people engaged with the Sacred Heart. It was no longer a bloody device signaling penitential suffering, but a gentle, inviting portrait of a benign savior who welcomed an intimate relationship with the devotee, and in less visceral terms than

Batoni's influential image."[51] This shift in imagery, now more sympathetic than empathetic,[52] moves the focus away from the painful intimacy and personal abandonment of Margaret Mary's visions. The newer icon of the Sacred Heart points more generally to the tender and reassuring love of Jesus that "informs" the heart, thereby transposing devotion from the visceral organ to the Divine Person.[53]

That transposition came to be solidified in the proliferation of life-sized statues that gave public recognition to the Sacred Heart. Portraying Jesus in a standing pose, with full-length robes, outstretched arms, open hands, and a solemn demeanor, the new statuary of "the welcoming Savior" is "one of intimate revelation grounded ultimately in the experience of Alacoque, but now presented for everyone in clearly pastoral terms of comforting acceptance and support. The mystical revelation, couched in suffering and extreme experience, has become a universal message of consolation."[54]

Today, whether for public worship or private devotion, depictions of the Sacred Heart continue to communicate the realism of divine love for humanity. On the one hand, the Sacred Heart remains a devotional icon, an image that, according to ancient tradition, "participates in the being of its original by virtue of looking like it." On the other hand, the Sacred Heart serves as a

---

[51] Morgan, *Sacred Heart of Jesus*, 23.

[52] "As a more pastoral version of the devotion, sympathy posits an affinity or inclination between Jesus and the soul, but does not aim at canceling their difference in the destruction of the self." Morgan, "Rhetoric of the Heart," 97–98.

[53] Morgan, *Sacred Heart of Jesus*, 24–26.

[54] Morgan, *Sacred Heart of Jesus*, 32.

spiritual symbol, representing, in the words of Pope Pius XII, "that threefold love [divine, human, and sensible] with which the divine Redeemer unceasingly loves His eternal Father and all mankind." In either case, the depiction of this sacred image points to the source of transformation for the contemporary world. As Pope St. John Paul II asserted, "The faithful still need to be guided to contemplate adoringly the mystery of Christ, the God-Man, in order to become men and women of interior life, people who feel and live the call to new life, to holiness, to reparation, which is apostolic cooperation in the salvation of the world."[55]

In the Salesian tradition, this mystery of redemptive intimacy — "Behold this Heart, which has so loved men" — serves as a focal point for the devout life when one learns to engage divine love and mercy through mental prayer.

A Salesian Method of Meditation

A renowned spiritual director, St. Francis de Sales understood well the power of prayer. A master of mystical theology, he taught people in various states in life the art of praying, introducing the rudiments to some and advancing the skills of others. In every case, his spiritual counsel accentuated the work of a spiritual imagination.

The Salesian Imagination[56]

St. Francis de Sales knew from personal experience the creative or productive power of the imagination — its capacity to yield new

---

[55] Cited in Morgan, "Rhetoric of the Heart," 110.

[56] This section draws extensively from my chapter on "Playful Prayer: Imagination and the Task of Theology in a Salesian Perspective," in *Salesian Spirituality: Catalyst to Collaboration*, ed. William Ruhl (Washington, DC: De Sales School of Theology, 1993), 169–188.

cognitive insights, generate newfound feeling, and stir up novel approaches to living in this world. Profoundly influenced by the beauty of his native Savoy, he stands out among religious authors of the seventeenth century due to the remarkable style of his writings. These contain so many images — "not only one word images, but also extended metaphors and allegories, personifications, comparisons so characteristic of [him], symbols and parables" — that his spiritual advice takes on a decidedly imaginative character. Far more than an affectatious flair, his style provokes thought and evokes the Spirit through images that "reflect his thought, his heart, and his entire being."[57]

No doubt, the Jesuit education the saint received contributed to the flowering of his imagination. In contrast to the artistic caution of the Reformation, with its penchant for eliminating ecclesiastical sounds and colors as not reflecting the sinful nature of human beings, Francis experienced a different intellectual milieu, especially during his years of schooling in Paris. There, under the tutelage of Gilbert Génébrard, Francis studied the biblical Canticle of Canticles. Rich with symbolic meaning, this work of divine revelation transformed his view of human and divine relationships; as one of his biographers rightly notes, "From that time, he was no longer able to conceive of the spiritual life except as a love story, the most beautiful of love stories."[58]

---

[57] Henri Lemaire, *Étude des images littéraires de François de Sales* (Paris: A.-G. Nizet, 1969), 15–16, 129. Lemaire estimates that the saint used approximately thirty-three thousand images in the complete corpus of his writings!

[58] André Ravier, S.J., *Francis de Sales: Sage and Saint* (San Francisco: Ignatius Press, 1988), 31.

That newfound, imaginative appreciation of the spiritual life later found its way into Francis's own preaching and his instructions on the subject. Known throughout his homeland for the sacred eloquence with which he preached,[59] Francis's talks were filled with illustrations and comparisons drawn from Sacred Scripture, natural history, and the whole range of human action. More than mere ornamentation, the use of images served an epistemological and existential purpose, for they possess "an inestimable efficacy to enlighten the mind and move the will" (*On the Preacher and Preaching*, 50).

For St. Francis de Sales, the imagination also served an essential role in the life of prayer, because it enables the lively and attentive realization of God's presence. As the saint explains:

> Although faith assures of his presence, yet because we do not seek him with our eyes we often forget about him and behave as if God were far distant from us. We really know that he is present in all things, but because we do not reflect on that fact we act as if we did not know it. This is why before praying we must always arouse our souls to explicit thought and consideration of God's presence. (*Introduction*, 2:2)

The power of imagination, which produces a conscious aware-ness of the divine, in turn helps us to formulate our response to God's presence as manifested in our world. Locating the spiritual faculty of the imagination not simply in the mind but in the heart, St. Francis de Sales thereby fashioned a holistic vision regarding the Christian life. As the editors of the saint's letters point out:

[59] See Dom Henry Mackey, *St. Francis de Sales as Preacher: A Study*, trans. Thomas Dailey (Bangalore: Indian Institute of Spirituality, 1992).

At the root of his perception, and at the deepest point of wisdom of Salesian spirituality, is the assumption, which derives in part from the Christian humanist tradition, that the spiritual life is not primarily about understanding, nor solely a matter of enthusiasm. It is a dynamic, integrative process that is brought about through the engagement of the whole person. The heart in Salesian thought is the seat both of intellect and of will. There the affective as well as cognitive capacities of the person are seen to dwell. All Salesian praxis then proceeds from this conceptual point of view. (*Letters of Spiritual Direction*, 57–58)

This mutually cognitive and affective approach informs the mystique of Salesian spirituality. In this tradition, we seek not simply to know God but to be joined with His infinite goodness. More mystical than speculative, this focus brings us into the "imaginative" realm of meditation and contemplation. In so praying with and before the Sacred Heart, we can appreciate the saint's claim that "love is the abridgment of all theology" (*Treatise*, 8:1).

Steeped in the Salesian way of prayer, St. Margaret Mary would come to embody the mysticism championed by the co-founders of the Visitation Order. As Wendy Wright explains, she knew firsthand the tradition of imagining the divine in bodily form, which was coupled with the practice of depicting the embodied God, especially in Jesus' death on the Cross.

This practice is not simply literary or artistic. It is performative as well. Within the contemplative/meditative streams of Christian life that might well be termed "embodied mysticism." Devotees have not only gazed upon God's embodiment, they have entered that body in prayer and explored it. Especially have they enjoyed an intimacy with the body's apertures, the wounds, and with the divine Heart revealed by entry into those wounds.[60]

That prayerfully intimate experience reached its apex in St. Margaret Mary's "exchange of hearts" with the Savior. Through her union with the Sacred Heart, which Jesus manifested to her, this Visitation nun came to fulfill the exhortation of St. Francis de Sales for all who pray, namely, that "devout souls should not have any heart but His, no will but His, no other affections or desires than His, in short, they must be completely in Him."[61]

United to God in this thoroughgoing way, St. Margaret Mary underwent a personal transformation. Through prayer, she came to what Wright calls a "catalyzing and focusing of all her life energies into a single amorous pursuit," the expression of which was her consecration to the Sacred Heart and subsequent devotion to it. From her prayer, St. Margaret Mary communicated to the world the ultimate meaning of this divine Heart:

> Love was its meaning. Love was the basic fabric of a merciful universe in which pain was transfigured into joy. Love was at once the beginning and end point and the point at which all beings converge. In the most intimate recess of the divine life is discovered this fearful and wonderful secret.[62]

To arouse that desire for love and union with God, and to discover its secret in the Sacred Heart of Jesus—this is the ultimate purpose of meditation or mental prayer in the Salesian tradition. We may not share St. Margaret Mary's profound mystical

---

[60] Wright, "Inside My Body," 186.

[61] Cited in Wright, "Inside My Body," 190-191.

[62] Wright, "A Wide and Fleshy Love," 268.

experience, but St. Francis de Sales does offer us a way to enter into this meditative or contemplative prayer.[63] In the second part of his *Introduction to the Devout Life*, he outlines the steps by which anyone can practice this typically monastic form of prayer.

The Salesian Structure of Mental Prayer [64]

Prayer in the Salesian tradition is a matter of both mind and heart. Conceived as a form of inspired imagining, it focuses more on listening to God than on speaking to God (as one would do in vocal prayer). When that meditative attentiveness is focused on the Sacred Heart, we can grow in both our understanding of the Savior's love and in our desire to respond to it in our lives.

St. Francis de Sales's method for meditation begins with intentional preparation. Because we do not actually see God, Francis counsels us first to draw our minds briefly to a consideration of God's never-ending *presence*, so as to evoke a sense of prayerful reverence. This we can do by any of four means that he suggests:

> The first consists of a lively, attentive realization of God's absolute presence, that is, that God is in all things and all places....

---

[63] St. Francis de Sales distinguishes meditation from thought, which is the musing of the mind, and from study, whose goal is to learn (*Treatise*, 6:2). He then explains how meditation differs from contemplation inasmuch as the former is a consideration of the divine mystery undertaken in a somewhat painstaking and detailed manner, while the latter is a more collective view of the divine that requires no labor to behold (*Treatise*, 6:3-5).

[64] This section draws extensively from chapter 11 of my book *Live Today Well: St. Francis de Sales's Simple Approach to Holiness* (Manchester, NH: Sophia Institute Press, 2015).

The second way ... is to remember that he is not only in the place where you are but also that he is present in a most particular manner in your heart and in the very center of your spirit....

A third way is to consider how our Savior in his humanity gazes down from heaven on all mankind ... and most especially on those who are at prayer, whose actions and conduct he observes....

A fourth method consists in use of simple imagination when we represent to ourselves the Savior in his sacred humanity as if he were near us, just as we sometimes imagine a friend to be present. (*Introduction*, 2:2)

When it comes to devotion to the Sacred Heart, the fourth method in particular invites us to call to mind the reality that the Savior's Heart is present to us, just as it was really present to St. Margaret Mary in her contemplative experience.

After invoking God's help to hear His holy inspirations, we then enter into the "*mystery*" that draws our attention. By this, St. Francis de Sales means that we use our imagination to focus upon a particular scenario in which the Sacred Heart is revealed. By carefully reading the relevant biblical story and picturing ourselves present then and there, we enter into the event and focus our minds on the manifestation of the Sacred Heart. By envisioning the reality of the divine mystery before us, we use our imagination to make the sacred moment present again and are thus drawn into an experience of the Sacred Heart's activity in our own lives.

With that mystery in mind, we then allow the Holy Spirit to guide us from thought to feeling to action. By an act of the mind, we give *consideration* to one or more thoughts about the scene we are picturing. What do we see going on there? What is happening in terms of encountering the Lord? What words ring out and draw our attention? What do we think about the event being narrated and, even more importantly, about the Heart of Jesus acting there? How do we see ourselves in reliving that moment?

In the Salesian approach to prayer, these or similar considerations are intended to excite in us a sense of the holy, an *affection* in our hearts that has been inspired by the Sacred Heart. St. Francis de Sales enumerates the possible feelings we may have as a result of these considerations:

> Love of God and neighbor, desire for heaven and glory, zeal for the salvation of souls, imitation of the life of our Lord, compassion, awe, joy, fear of God's displeasure, judgment, and hell, hatred of sin, confidence in God's goodness and mercy, and deep sorrow for the sins of our past life. (*Introduction*, 2:6)

Whatever the type of affection, the point here is to allow our hearts to be moved by the divine Heart and to cultivate our own desire and passion for union with God, not unlike what St. Margaret Mary experienced in the Lord's apparitions to her. Being so inspired by Him to whom we aspire, we will thereby be moved to act in accord with the divine will.

The final step is essential to the devotion. Mysticism, for St. Francis de Sales, is not an abstraction, not simply a thought or a feeling. Mental prayer is meant to transform our lives! Thus, Salesian meditation always includes a *resolution*, a decision to embody or put into practice the inspirations received by acting in determinate ways that align our human reality with the divine mystery about which we prayed.

Presence, mystery, consideration, affection, and resolution—these are the "imaginative" elements of meditation in the Salesian tradition, not in the sense of fanciful abstractions but in the manner of experiencing the supernatural as it is manifested to us and within us through the grace of the Sacred Heart. To weave the grace of this inspiration into the fabric of our lives, or even to supply for it on those days when other responsibilities preclude our having sufficient time for mental prayer, St. Francis de Sales offers two related counsels. The first implores us to gather a "spiritual bouquet" from our prayer, which he describes in this charming way:

> People who have been walking about in a beautiful garden do not like to leave without gathering in their hands four or five flowers to smell and keep for the rest of the day. In the same way, when our soul has carefully considered by meditation a certain mystery we should select one, two, or three points that we liked best and that are most adapted to our improvement, think frequently about them, and smell them spiritually during the rest of the day. (*Introduction*, 2:7)

By culling some holy flowers, particularly a word or thought that we can associate with the image of the Sacred Heart, we are able to recall, and thus reactivate, the affections that our prayerful encounter with the Lord has stirred in us. This we can readily do in our minds and hearts even while we are busy with the other activities of the day.

The second imaginative exercise is the making of aspirations. These are simple thoughts or brief sayings that we can meditatively call to mind in association with our daily experiences. By making aspirations concerning the Sacred Heart throughout the day, we pray even when we are busy with other things for which we are responsible.

Through the exercise of mental prayer, we come to experience the world of interconnected hearts of which St. Francis de

Sales speaks. As artists communicate meaning and inspire wonder through a visual medium, so persons at prayer make use of the imagination to envision the divine mystery and respond to its inspiration in their hearts and souls. By means of this prayerful imagining, "We retire into God before we aspire to him, and we aspire to him so that we may retire into him" (*Introduction*, 3:13). Habituating ourselves to the Sacred Heart in this way allows us to commune with Jesus now, as a foretaste of that union of hearts we seek to enjoy eternally.

Part 3

A Salesian Novena

✠

MEDITATIONS ON THE
SACRED HEART OF JESUS

The invitation to "behold this Heart" draws us to an exercise of prayerful devotion, which we here propose. Grounded in the Salesian tradition of interconnected hearts and guided by the Salesian vision of inspiration through mental prayer, this "novena" offers nine meditations on the Sacred Heart of Jesus. These spiritual colloquies look to various aspects of the Sacred Heart as these are revealed in the biblical chronology of Jesus' life.

While the "visualist paradigm" of devotion to the Sacred Heart typically highlights sketched, painted, or sculpted images, the pictures proposed here as a basis for meditation are entirely narrative. The images are drawn from what Pope Francis calls the "story of stories"—the texts of Sacred Scripture that narrate "the great love story between God and humanity." All good stories, the pope says, "influence our lives ... leave their mark on us ... shape our convictions and our behavior ... [and] help us understand and communicate who we are." The biblical narratives, in particular, demonstrate a unique power to inspire by enabling us to see that "God has become personally woven into our humanity, and so has given us a new way of weaving our stories."[65]

The nine meditations that follow draw their inspiration from the Gospel narratives of the life, death, and Resurrection of Jesus. From each story we draw out elements that contribute to the revelation of the Sacred Heart and highlight a key biblical term that focuses attention on a particular aspect of that revelation. We then supplement the narrative intelligence of the Gospel tale with related thoughts from the tradition of Salesian spirituality, drawn primarily from the writings of St. Francis de Sales. In turn, these biblical and Salesian texts provide the basis for an exercise of mental prayer, which is suggested through a series of considerations, affections, resolutions, and recollections.

These meditative chapters are intended to assist the reader with prayer to the Sacred Heart of Jesus. As St. Francis de Sales notes, prayer that centers on the life and Passion of our Lord is especially advantageous, because

> by often turning your eyes on him in meditation, your whole soul will be filled with him. You will learn his ways and form your actions after the pattern of his. He is "the

[65] Cited in Thomas Dailey, "Preaching the 'Story of Stories,'" *Homiletic and Pastoral Review*, February 26, 2020, https://www.hprweb.com/2020/02/preaching-the-story-of-stories. The article quotes from and analyzes the pope's 2019 Apostolic Letter *Aperuit Illis* instituting the Sunday of the Word of God, and his 2020 Message for World Communications Day ("'That you may tell your children and grandchildren' (Exod. 10:2): Life becomes history").

light of the world" (John 8:12), and therefore it is in him and by him and for him that we must be instructed and enlightened.... Finally, just as little children learn to speak by listening to their mothers and lisping words with them, so also by keeping close to our Savior in meditation and observing his words, actions, and affections we learn by his grace to speak, act, and will like him. (*Introduction*, 2:1)

Nevertheless, as the wise Doctor reminded those he directed, inspiration is ultimately a gift of the Holy Spirit. As such, he reminds us that we enjoy a true "liberty of the spirit" in living the devout life, especially in matters of prayer.[66] Consequently, the reader at prayer should not feel constrained by the specific thoughts or orderly progress proposed in these meditations. Other considerations may come to mind. Different affections may arise in the heart. More personally advantageous resolutions and recollections may be adopted. The meditations below offer a guide, but, as the saint says, we should follow the promptings of the Lord wherever He chooses to lead.

In this novena,[67] our hope is to aid the reader in learning from Him who is "gentle and humble of heart"—a particularly salient image for this devotion to the Sacred Heart and the most cherished image of Jesus in the Salesian tradition, which will inform the conclusion to this work.

---

[66] See Dailey, *Live Today Well*, 137-138.

[67] Traditionally, the novena takes place on the nine days leading up to the solemnity of the Most Sacred Heart of Jesus, which is celebrated on the Friday after the solemnity of Corpus Christi. As a prayerful devotion, however, the novena can be celebrated in any sequence of nine days—for example, the first nine days of the month, nine consecutive days in June (the month of the Sacred Heart), or the first Friday of the month for nine consecutive months.

The Pulsing Heart of Jesus
ON THE JOY OF THE INCARNATION

-|-

*Our narrative exposition of the Sacred Heart of Jesus
begins with the biblical mystery that gave rise to the
Order of the Visitation and the spiritual tradition in
which St. Margaret Mary Alacoque was immersed.
In the sacred tale of the encounter between Mary
and Elizabeth, we reflect on the first recognition of
the joy that the Sacred Heart brings to the world.*

THE VISITATION, *BY GERÓNIMO
ANTONIO DE EZQUERRA (CA. 1737)*

Luke 1:39–47

In those days Mary arose and went with haste into the hill
country, to a town in Judah, and she entered the house of
Zechariah and greeted Elizabeth. And when Elizabeth heard
the greeting of Mary, the baby leaped in her womb. And
Elizabeth was filled with the Holy Spirit, and she exclaimed

with a loud cry, "Blessed are you among women, and blessed is the fruit of your womb! And why is this granted to me that the mother of my Lord should come to me? For behold, when the sound of your greeting came to my ears, the baby in my womb leaped for joy. And blessed is she who believed that there would be a fulfillment of what was spoken to her from the Lord." And Mary said, "My soul magnifies the Lord, and my spirit rejoices in God my Savior."

Biblical Narration

Those days, for Mary, have been a whirlwind unlike any she, or anyone else in human history, had ever known. She has only recently been visited by the angel Gabriel, who announced to her the divine intention that she give birth to the Son of God. When she wondered how that could be, she was reminded that with God, all things were possible. As a sign of that truth, she was told the news that her elderly relative was, in fact, six months pregnant, by the grace of God. When Mary then acquiesced to God's will for her, she experienced the Spirit-induced generation of new life in her virginal womb. The Sacred Heart began to pulse.

Still awed at the divine disclosure now coming to life in her, she sets out *with haste* to visit Elizabeth. She is eager to see for herself the marvelous wonder about which the angel spoke. She seeks to help a relative in need. She desires to share her own astonishment with perhaps the only one who will understand that these stupendous happenings have a divine origin. The good news impels her to go forth promptly, with no hesitation about making such an arduous, even dangerous, three-day journey *into the hill country*.

When the unlikely mothers meet, the mystery makes itself known. With nothing but a *sound of greeting*, the hearts of the pre-born children "speak" to each other. He who years later will announce the coming of the Lord now *leaps for joy in his mother's womb*. His mother feels it. She also knows the cause. That fetal movement, in conjunction with the movement of the *Holy Spirit*, stirs Elizabeth to recognize in a new light the one who stands in the threshold—the *blessed* one in whose womb is the One who will bless the world as its *Lord* and Savior. Astonishment gives way to embrace.

From that embrace exultation arises. Far beyond the moment and the miracle in which these two women inexplicably find themselves participating, Mary comprehends the greater meaning of what is happening. She may not have known all that would transpire in the life of her Son, but she realized then that through her, the *Lord's* promise to His chosen people would come to fulfillment. Her *soul*, her *spirit*, her whole being, rightly *rejoices*. From her own heart, the lyrical verses of the Magnificat ring out with profound praise for the coming-to-be of the Sacred Heart within her.

The greetings between Elizabeth and Mary at the Visitation give voice to the gospel. The heart-to-heart encounter between these two mothers, and between the children within them, sets salvation history on its new and definitive course. The two women would go about their maternal activity without elaboration for the next *three months*, until the nativity of John the Baptist. Then the Blessed Mother would return home to prepare herself for the greatest Nativity of all—the birth of God's only-begotten Son and the coming of the Sacred Heart into the world.

"Leaping for Joy"

For us, this is a familiar figure of speech, but the Greek word that Luke used (σκιρτάω) refers to an actual experience, one literally felt by Elizabeth when John *leaped* in her womb. "Quickening" fetal movements are typical in any pregnancy and play an essential role in a child's development. But this incidence is extraordinary, more than a mere coincidence in its timing, and Elizabeth recognizes its cause and interprets its meaning. As the narration makes clear in its repetition, her preborn son leaps in her womb because of the presence of the Christ Child. The Sacred Heart, pulsing nearby, induces joy in those whom Jesus encounters.

Salesian Spirituality

The mystery narrated in the biblical Visitation represents the central axis around which the worldview of St. Francis de Sales revolves and provides the foundation on which the Salesian tradition of theology and spirituality develops.[68] The Gospel tale sums up all the Christian mysteries as expressing the dynamics of love by way of a divine-human encounter.[69] The embrace between Elizabeth and Mary—leading to a leap of joy and a song of exultation—portrays in visible manner the invisible "kiss" by which "the God of the human heart" visits His people in the person of His Beloved Son and initiates "His redemptive mission of communion with human hearts."[70]

---

[68] "The mystery of the Visitation fundamentally marks the reading of the world that Saint Francis de Sales has, his theology, his spirituality, and also certain peculiarities of his style and his speech; in this way the cohesion of his thought is revealed: against the contrary assertion, the most common, a precise doctrine structures his reasoning and the expression which he gives to it, at the same time as it founds a tradition, or revivifies it, even giving it a new face." Bordes, "La méditation du mystère de la Visitation," 69.

[69] See Wright, *Heart Speaks to Heart*, 38.

[70] Joseph Chorpenning, "The Dynamics of Divine Love: Francis de Sales's Picturing of the Biblical Mystery of the Visitation," in *Ut pictura amor: The Reflexive Imagery of Love in Artistic Theory and Practice*,

In two sermons for the feast of the Visitation (given in 1618 and 1621), St. Francis de Sales explores the dynamic of love at work in the biblical scene. Beginning with movement, the narrative speaks of the essence of love, which is to go out of oneself toward, and for the sake of, the other. "Charity is never idle," says the saint, and Mary's "ardent charity" and "profound humility" prompt her to make this visitation (*Sermons on Our Lady*, 50).

Upon Mary's arrival at her destination, grace flows from the Heart of the child Jesus incarnate within her, such that "the whole house was overcome with joy" (*Sermons on Our Lady*, 58) and those within it are transformed. Elizabeth is profoundly humbled, confirms her faith in God as the source of all graces, and experiences "interior conversion, the change to a better life" when her baby leaps for joy in her womb (*Sermons on Our Lady*, 166). For his part, John "was sanctified in his mother's womb" and "filled with wisdom and the knowledge of God and divine mysteries." He "must have recognized the Saviour in the womb of Our Lady," says the saint, "since at His arrival he leapt for joy in his mother's womb; he must also have loved Him, for we do not leap for joy over the coming of those we neither know nor love" (*Sermons on Our Lady*, 161).

The knowledge and love of Jesus experienced by John in the womb continue to be sources of transforming grace and joy for all who encounter the Sacred Heart. What St. Francis exclaims to the Visitandines should resonate with all of us:

> Oh, my very dear Sisters, how you should be overwhelmed with joy when you are visited by this Divine Saviour in the Most Blessed Sacrament of the Altar, and by the interior

1500–1700, eds. Walter S. Melion, Joanna Woodall, and Michael Zell (Leiden, Netherlands: Brill, 2017), 507.

69

graces which you receive daily from His Divine Majesty through the many inspirations and words which He speaks to your hearts.... What thanksgiving you owe to this Lord for so many favors! With what careful attention you should listen to Him, and how faithfully and promptly you should do His divine will! (*Sermons on Our Lady*, 59)

And from that insight, the practice of the devout life follows:

O my dear Sisters ... what zeal you should have in imitating her [Our Lady], especially her charity and humility, which were the chief virtues which urged her to make this visitation. You should therefore be particularly distinguished in their practice, which will move you to go with haste and joy to visit your sick sisters, cordially helping and serving one another in your infirmities, whether they be spiritual or corporal. And whenever there is an opportunity of practicing humility and charity you ought to do so with a special care and promptness. (*Sermons on Our Lady*, 60)

Prayerful Inspiration

In light of this biblical mystery and informed by St. Francis de Sales's preaching about it, we can also encounter the God of the human heart through the "visitation" that takes place in our prayer to the Sacred Heart of Jesus.

Considerations

1. Reflect on the generation of human life and how it comes into being daily around the world. See, as Mary and Elizabeth did, that this happens through the grace of God. Consider the novelty of each human being, conceived through

the self-giving of man and woman and shaped by their genetic gift into a one-of-a-kind person. Marvel at the pulsing heart made visible on a sonogram, or the rhythmic beating of your own heart.

2. Consider your distinct place in the long legacy of human generations. Coming into being at a particular time in history and place in the world, you are the unique child of your parents, as they were of theirs, with a potential all your own. So, too, you may have (or already have had) the amazing opportunity to share new life by bringing a child unlike any other into the world. Recognize that in every human life a child of God comes to be, and that this happens through a perfect correspondence between the abundance and inclination of the Creator to bestow life, and the great desire and capacity to receive that life on the part of humanity (*Treatise*, 1:15).

3. Ponder the grace of life that breathes within your own heart and soul. Elizabeth felt that grace in her son's movement within her. Today, grace also moves you, pulsing with life in each beat of your heart. Your heart feels the impulse to love, is moved to live a good life with and for others, and receives from the Holy Spirit the inspirations that guide that good life.

Affections

1. Arouse in your heart a profound gratitude for the gift of life that you have been given. You have been blessed with this gift, blessed by the God who created you and by those whose care has formed you into the person you are. Be thankful.

2. Humble yourself with the realization that you had nothing to do with coming to be in this world! Rather, you have

been willed into existence by a loving God. Like Mary, acknowledge that your life proceeds from the fact that God has looked upon you who are otherwise merely a "lowly servant."

3. Stir within your heart a joyful exultation at the graces of God still at work within you. Your distinct features and traits, your particular gifts and talents—all are favors from the Lord. Cultivate a desire to share your gifts with others, as Mary did with Elizabeth.

Salesian Devotion

Invoking the example of the Blessed Mother, St. Francis de Sales reminds us in his preaching: "If then we wish to prove that we do indeed love God, and if we wish others to believe us when we assure them of this, we must love our brothers [and sisters] well, serve them and assist them in their necessities." After all, "transformation is the true mark of a divine visitation" (*Sermons on Our Lady*, 159, 170).

Resolutions

1. On a *personal* level, what might you do for your family? Your place there has been affected by generations past; in turn, you will affect generations to come. Perhaps you could spend some quality time visiting or conversing with those who have come before you. You might also dedicate time to be with your own children or relatives, perhaps sharing a family story with them that will give joy to your whole house.

2. On a *relational* level, what might you do in terms of the ordinary "visitations" that occur daily? Perhaps you could strive to be more welcoming to those who come to you

throughout the day. You might simply offer a friendly smile or cordial greeting, or you could extend an invitation to a neighbor to visit your house. Remembering that "charity is never idle," perhaps you could visit someone and lend a helping hand.

3. On a *societal* level, what might you do to practice "ardent charity" and "profound humility" in the joyful service of others? Perhaps you could support the work of pro-life movements, or serve an organization that assists expectant or new mothers, or volunteer with a related parish program.

Recollections

1. In adoration before the Lord, give thanks for the gift of your life and the sustaining presence of God in your heart.

2. Remember the inspirations you received in this meditation by calling to mind the song of Mary and sharing in her exultation with your own "leap" for joy.

3. Recall throughout the day this Salesian maxim: it is wonderful how attractive a gentle, pleasant manner is, and how much it wins hearts (*Introduction*, 3:26).

The Beloved Heart of Jesus
ON THE PRIMACY OF LOVING RELATIONSHIP

✠

Our narrative exposition of the Sacred Heart shifts to the onset of Jesus' public ministry. In the story of His Baptism, later confirmed at the Transfiguration, the Sacred Heart is revealed to be "beloved" by God the Father.

THE BAPTISM OF CHRIST,
BY ANTOINE COYPEL (CA. 1690)

Mark 1:9–11
In those days Jesus came from Nazareth of Galilee and was baptized by John in the Jordan. And when he came up out of the water, immediately he saw the heavens being torn open and the Spirit descending on him like a dove. And a voice came from heaven, "You are my beloved Son; with you I am well pleased."

Behold This Heart

Matthew 17:1–9

And after six days Jesus took with him Peter and James, and John his brother, and led them up a high mountain by themselves. And he was transfigured before them, and his face shone like the sun, and his clothes white as light. And behold, there appeared to them Moses and Elijah, talking with him. And Peter said to Jesus, "Lord, it is good that we are here. If you wish, I will make three tents here, one for you and one for Moses and one for Elijah." He was still speaking when, behold, a bright cloud overshadowed them, and a voice from the cloud said, "This is my beloved Son, with him I am well pleased; listen to him." When the disciples heard this, they fell on their faces and were terrified. But Jesus came and touched them, saying, "Rise, and have no fear." And when they lifted up their eyes, they saw no one but Jesus only. And as they were coming down the mountain, Jesus commanded them, "Tell no one the vision, until the Son of Man is raised from the dead."

Biblical Narration

Having grown in wisdom and knowledge with His Holy Family, Jesus sets out on the course of His public ministry. He comes onto the scene to be *baptized by John*—His relative, the one who "leaped for joy" when they were both still in the womb. Joining others *in the Jordan* River, Jesus is set apart for His life's work with a supernatural experience, a "theophany" in which God is manifest in sight and sound. The *voice from heaven* speaks directly to Him, with a divine assurance that equips Him for the mission ahead.

In that mission, as in every human life, ups and downs abound. He speaks with surpassing wisdom and authority, often clashing with prevailing mindsets. He performs miraculous cures and signs, which are met with incredulity. He gathers followers and teaches them about the Messiah, proposing a new way of life almost too hard to bear.

Along the way, He tells His disciples that He will be killed in Jerusalem. Now they are making their way to that religious capital. Having been walking, silently, for *six days*, we can only imagine what they were thinking. Confused by what they have seen, not yet sure who this Jesus is, and wondering why He would have to die, the disciples were likely quite somber.

Unexpectedly, Jesus takes three of them—*Peter and James and John*—on a detour. They go off *by themselves*, away from the cacophony of the crowds and the musings of the many. They go up a *high mountain*, which their religious tradition held to be a place of sacred significance. The mountaintop is where divinity meets humanity (as in the story of Moses) and radically changes history.

What happens next defies description! The disciples get a glimpse of glory as Jesus is *transfigured before them*. What they see must be overwhelming. Jesus' appearance—*white as the light of the sun*—sends a shock to their system. Probably squinting in the brightness, they also saw *Moses and Elijah*—two of the greatest figures in the Hebrew Scriptures, representatives of the entire Law and all the prophets—chatting with the Master. The disciples surely felt immersed in a religious experience like no other. *Peter* suggests, perhaps only semiconsciously, that they build some *tents* so they can stay right where they are.

But sacred stasis is not to be. Without warning, they are *overshadowed by a bright cloud*, enveloped in a heavenly mystery about to be revealed to them. A voice speaks from above with words that reiterate what was proclaimed at Jesus' Baptism but are now directed to the disciples: *"This is my Son, the Beloved"*—the same One with whom God is *well pleased*. This time, the voice adds a command—"*Listen to Him!*"—though without reference to what they are supposed to hear.

The stupendous sights and sounds are too much to bear. Having nowhere to run, the disciples can only *fall on their faces* to the ground. They are overcome by fright, *terrified* by the strange occurrences and their understanding that according to their tradition, a direct encounter with God means certain death.

Yet mortal reckoning does not come. Instead, *Jesus comes* to their side. By touching them, he makes this supernatural event real. He tells them again to *have no fear*. Perhaps now they will trust Him. But He also foretells being *raised from the dead*, which probably confuses them even more!

"The Beloved One"

Narrated as moments of mystical awareness, the two revelations of Jesus as the Son of God the Father situate His identity squarely in the realm of sacred hearts. Beyond affirming that Jesus shares His nature, the Father lays claim to the Son as "the Beloved One" (ἀγαπητός), a title that expresses unparalleled esteem, favored status, and preeminent worth.

As "the Beloved," Jesus is defined and characterized from all eternity by a relationship of profound affection, a union of hearts with the God who is His Father. This claim, announced with authority from on high, is made before Jesus undertakes His public ministry (at His Baptism), and is made again (at the Transfiguration) before the fulfillment of His mission in Jerusalem.

In the Sacred Heart, we discover the primacy of relationship over action. Jesus is the Son of God, beloved by His Father prior to and independent of what He says and does on earth. Eternally united in divine affection, their hearts beat as one. From that

Sacred Heart will come the acts by which divine love is demonstrated for all humanity.

Salesian Spirituality

Like the disciples, we need heavenly insight to understand the great mystery at the heart of life's journey. When we realize in faith who Jesus is and learn to listen to Him, we can begin to appreciate what is shone forth for us so brilliantly in the Sacred Heart of the Beloved Son. We listen to Him best, says St. Francis de Sales, when we pray, for "it is truly by means of prayer that one approaches perfection" (*Oeuvres*, 9:28).

Prayer invites us to tap into that primordial relation of divine affection in order to see and to hear what God knows and desires for us. To pray is to participate, in a limited way, in the Transfiguration experience, which for St. Francis de Sales was less a miracle than the cessation of a miracle. The true miracle is the Incarnation, wherein the eternal state of God's superior glory is subsumed under the mortal condition of our inferior humanity, with its miseries, pains, and sufferings. "At the hour of the Transfiguration," the saint preaches, "this miracle ceases for a time, Our Lord letting his inferior part delight in the glory and consolation of his superior part" (*Oeuvres*, 9:28). The Sacred Heart dwelling within the human body of Jesus shines forth in the dazzling brightness of Him who glories in being loved.

That glory, to which we are also destined, remains ineffable. The glory of God cannot be plainly understood on account of its infinity. Yet, the saint says, as the disciples caught a glimpse of His glory on the mountaintop, so prayer enables us to know something of it, to have the hope of it.[71] For the disciples on that

---

[71] These ideas appear in the saint's plan for a sermon for the second Sunday of Lent on February 19, 1617. *Oeuvres*, 8: 276-279.

mountaintop and those who contemplate Him in prayer, Jesus "shows us a spark of eternal glory and a drop of that ocean, of that sea of incomparable felicity, to make us desire it in its entirety" (*Sermons for Lent*, 58).

Drawn by that desire in prayer, especially prayer to the Sacred Heart of Jesus, we are called to hear the divine voice as it speaks to us in the midst of both our consolations and our afflictions. For St. Francis de Sales, the latter speak more clearly to a union of hearts, for "there is nothing delectable" in the prayer of suffering. In any case, prayer is the work of every disciple, "for it is there, principally, where this divine Master speaks to us." In His speaking to us in prayer, "we learn to do well that which we must do." Nevertheless, "it will not do us any good to listen if we do not do what he says to us, observing faithfully his commandments and his wishes" (*Oeuvres*, 9:30).

Ultimately, prayer perfects us by teaching us to see the Lord in whatever we do. As St. Francis de Sales concludes, "The only thing necessary is to see God, to search only for him, to have no other affection than for him, and then we will be blessed. Souls which have attained this degree of perfection have an entirely particular care to look upon and to be held by Our Lord crucified on Calvary, because they find him there more alone than in any other place" (*Oeuvres*, 9:31). There, especially, the One who was affirmed and confirmed by a heavenly voice reveals the full character of His "beloved" Sacred Heart.

Prayerful Inspiration

As Peter, James, and John were commanded on the mountaintop to listen to the beloved Son, so we are called to unite our hearts to the Sacred Heart through meditative prayer.

Considerations

1. Reflect on the great mystery and journey of human life in the world and with its never-ending search for meaning. What sources of happiness bring you a sense of fulfillment? To what "voices" do you listen for guidance and direction?

2. Confront the prospect of your own death—with the attendant questions that plague each of us in this mortal state. Who or where is God? Does religious faith make a real difference? Do you approach your earthly demise with dread (as a defeat) or with hope (of future glory)?

3. Ponder the many ways in which God reveals Himself—in nature, in Sacred Scripture, in prayer. Do you "see" God on the mountaintops and in the valleys of life? Do you "hear" God in the reading or proclamation of His Word? Have you fulfilled well your Christian duty to be attentive to God's presence through prayer?

Affections

1. Arouse in yourself a holy fear of missing opportunities to follow the Lord and listen to His inspirations. The path up the mountain can be steep and rugged, and missteps make the journey more difficult. But at the top awaits an experience of glory!

2. Embrace in your heart the reality of being "beloved" by God. By virtue of your Baptism, you have been adopted as a son or daughter of the heavenly Father. That affirmation of divine esteem and affection initiates a relationship that precedes all your actions. The joyous fact is that we cannot do anything in this life to make God love us more than He already does! Take delight in hearing the voice of the Father.

3. Stir in your soul a desire to see the face of God, to enjoy the glory of heaven, to be united in the happiness of interconnected hearts. For that destiny you have been created; to that beatitude you are called. Here below you experience a foretaste of that eternal relationship through reception of Holy Communion, but heaven attracts us as "a place of consolation where all joys and blessings are found and experienced" (*Sermons for Lent*, 57).

Salesian Devotion

Preaching about the Transfiguration, St. Francis de Sales reminds us that "perfection itself is … to obey the Father and listen to the Son" (*Oeuvres*, 9:30). That perfection we can seek throughout each day's journey.

Resolutions

1. On a *personal* level, what might you do to cultivate an active prayer life as a foretaste of heavenly beatitude? Perhaps you could begin each day with a word of thanks to God for the gift of being alive! Or you might commend yourself to the Sacred Heart daily through a morning offering or evening thanksgiving. Or you could choose to participate in some opportunity for spiritual devotion at your parish outside of Sunday Mass (such as novenas or eucharistic adoration).

2. On a *relational* level, what might you do to see and treat others as having hearts "beloved" by God? We see His beloved in the elderly among us; you might offer to accompany an older neighbor or parishioner along his or her journey by taking him or her to church or out to breakfast. We must see as beloved even those with whom we have a challenging

relationship; perhaps you could find an opportunity to do that person an intentional act of kindness.

3. On a *societal* level, what might you do to ease the uphill climb that so many have to make in life? Perhaps you might be able to volunteer with organizations that work to prevent suicide or provide hospice care. Or you could simply contribute your time or treasure to local charities that assist those in dire straits.

Recollections

1. In adoration before the Lord, give thanks for the opportunity to glimpse His glory in the sacraments, especially in the celebration of Mass and the reception of Holy Communion.

2. Remember the inspirations you received in this meditation by recalling that voice of the Father affirming the Sacred Heart in His "beloved" Son and commanding us to "listen to Him" that we might also enjoy eternal beatitude.

3. Recall throughout the day this Salesian maxim: God has always been without beginning and without end, and so He has always loved you from all eternity (*Introduction*, 5:14).

MEDITATION 3

The Compassionate Heart of Jesus
ON THE DIVINE RESPONSE TO HUMAN NEED

⸻ ✙ ⸻

Our narrative exposition of the Sacred Heart of Jesus
looks to the interactions of Jesus with the crowds during
His public ministry. In these sacred tales, we encounter
the Sacred Heart in its loving response to those in need.

THE FEEDING OF THE MULTITUDE,
BY THE LIMBOURG BROTHERS (1411–1416)

Matthew 14:13–21

Now when Jesus heard [of the death of John the Baptist], he
withdrew from there in a boat to a desolate place by himself.
But when the crowds heard it, they followed him on foot
from the towns. When he went ashore he saw a great crowd,
and he had compassion and healed their sick. Now when

it was evening, the disciples came to him and said, "This is a desolate place, and the day is now over; send the crowds away to go into the villages and buy food for themselves." But Jesus said, "They need not go away; you give them something to eat." They said to him, "We have only five loaves here and two fish." And he said, "Bring them here to me." Then he ordered the crowds to sit down on the grass, and taking the five loaves and the two fish, he looked up to heaven and said a blessing. Then he broke the loaves and gave them to the disciples, and the disciples gave them to the crowds. And they all ate and were satisfied. And they took up twelve baskets full of the broken pieces left over. And those who ate were about five thousand men, besides women and children.

Biblical Narration

It must be difficult to be the Messiah!

Jesus will exercise the majority of His public ministry in Galilee, a small but densely populated region in Israel. There He has taken up His divinely appointed task of teaching and instructing His followers in the ways of faith. There He has undertaken His divinely empowered work of healing, working miracles for the blind, the leprous, and the possessed. There He is fulfilling His messianic mission of proclaiming the good news of the kingdom of God, describing its novel wonders through familiar parables.

And people are responding—in droves! Those searching for meaning find in Jesus a rabbi who speaks with unparalleled authority. Those seeking relief find in Him a wonder-worker and receive from Him the satisfaction of their needs. As He makes

His way through Galilee, the crowds following Him grow, as does their clamoring for more. His reputation begets great expectation. Yet the person working wonders in their midst is fully human, too. When He *hears* about the death of John the Baptist, His relative and precursor, He feels deeply the pain of losing a loved one. Now He must proclaim the kingdom alone. So He *withdraws* from the crowds as best He can—by taking off *in a boat* on the open lake known as the Sea of Galilee. In that *desolate place*, He can be *by Himself*, the solitary waters serving as a *place* of calm in which He can recenter Himself in view of the mission that remains ahead of Him. Yet this precious time alone will not last long.

The crowds *hear* that He is on the move. Word spreads quickly among the people in the towns. Impelled by their searching and seeking, roused by what they have seen and heard, they *follow* Him. They will not miss any opportunity to receive what they can from Him, even if it means making the journey *on foot* around the lake to await His arrival on the other side.

Imagine Jesus' surprise upon reaching the shore, where *He sees a great crowd* gathered to meet Him. Can they not leave Him alone for a while? Will they continue to demand more from Him?

He could resent their insistence. He could complain about their encroaching on His own time and space. He could be discouraged by their demands, made without any heed to who He really is.

Instead, He responds as He always does—from His Heart. He *has compassion* on them. He can sense their desperation. As an itinerant preacher, He knows what it means to walk on the road without stopping to eat. He can empathize with their hunger. He can sympathize with their pain. And He knows they are in need of more than they realize.

Out of this compassion, Jesus responds as only He can. He *heals their sick*. Later, He feeds them, miraculously providing such bounty that after the crowd *have eaten and are satisfied*, they are left with more food than they started with! The *five thousand men* and their families now have the strength needed to make their way home, there to realize that the deepest human need cannot be sated by this world's provisions.

"Having Compassion On"

While the miracle of feeding the multitude with just *five loaves and two fish* grabs our attention and elicits varying interpretations, what matters more to our spiritual appreciation is what motivated it. Here, as elsewhere in the Gospel, Jesus "*has compassion*" on those in need. Far more than simply feeling sorry for others, this compassion (from the Greek σπλαγχνίζομαι) refers to a yearning experience in one's inner organs, where the deepest affections were thought to be located. The spiritual need Jesus perceives evokes in Him a visceral response, which in turn inspires Him to alleviate the crowd's physical needs in miraculous ways that signal His messianic mission of curing the human spirit.

That mission continues. In the message revealed to St. Margaret Mary, and through her to all the world, the Sacred Heart "so impassioned with love" does not just have compassion; it is "nothing but love and mercy."

Salesian Spirituality

In the Salesian tradition, having compassion pertains to the first of the two chief exercises of sacred love, namely the "complacence" by which one sees the good in someone else and delights in it. The second exercise ("benevolence") follows from this when one chooses and acts to make that goodness grow.

As St. Francis de Sales describes it:

Compassion, sympathy, commiseration, or pity is simply an affection that makes us share the sufferings and sorrows of one we love and draw the misery he endures into our own heart. Hence it is called *misericordia*, as if we meant *misère de coeur*, misery of heart, just as complacence draws into a lover's heart the pleasure and contentment of the loved object.

He likens this love of complacence to the suffering that mothers experience because of the afflictions their children suffer. The most notable exemplar of this suffering is the Blessed Mother:

Alas, the same nails that crucified the body of that divine Child also crucified the soul of his Mother. The same thorns that pierced his head pierced through the soul of that all-sweet Mother. She felt the same miseries as her Son by commiseration, the same dolors by condolence, the same passion by compassion. In brief, the deadly sword that transpierced the body of that most beloved Son pierced through the heart of that most loving Mother. (*Treatise*, 5:4)

As Jesus had compassion for the needs of the crowds before Him, so we can cultivate a loving compassion when we reflect prayerfully upon the extent of His love for us, particularly in His Passion. Claiming that "love's beauty lies in the deformity of sorrow," St. Francis de Sales explains how our devotion to the Sacred Heart of Jesus draws this love into our hearts:

The loving complacence we have taken in our Savior's love makes the compassion we feel for his afflictions infinitely stronger, just as reciprocally when we pass back from compassion for his afflictions to complacence in love, our pleasure therein is far higher and more ardent. Thus both pain in love and love in pain are brought into being. (*Treatise*, 5:5)

In this way, compassion issues from and generates love. Just as Jesus had compassion for the crowds in need, so we see in His Sacred Heart "how much the Savior desires to enter into our souls by this love of dolorous complacence" (*Treatise*, 5:5).

Prayerful Inspiration

We experience complacence in love when we gaze inwardly in prayer, taking into our hearts the compassion the Sacred Heart has for our own needs and those of the people around us.

Considerations

1. Reflect upon the needs of the world. So many people suffer from poverty, hunger, disease, and other ills. Recall how the novel coronavirus has disrupted life around the world, leaving pain and death in its wake. Ponder the social and economic fallout from the pandemic that continues to cause global suffering. See how this misery unites humanity.

2. Consider what you "hunger" for in your own life. Acknowledge the needs you have—to be cared for, to be provided for, to be cured physically or emotionally. Examine the ways in which you seek to satisfy those needs. Reflect on how many of your needs have been met through the compassion and generosity of others—and the grace of God.

3. Look deeper into the "hunger" of your soul. You seek love that lasts. You search for happiness that endures. You hope

one day to reach heaven. Ask yourself what steps along the journey you are taking to find Him who alone can fulfill those needs.

Affections

1. Arouse in your heart a sympathetic love for those who suffer. See not simply statistics or data, but the real humanity of people whose stories make the daily news. Let the welfare of your friends and loved ones move you to condolence for the sorrows they are enduring.
2. Humble yourself at the suffering that results from the faults and failures in your own life. Honestly acknowledge the unhealthy habits that have brought about painful consequences for you. Pity the condition that your sins produce, while also realizing that the greater your misery is, the greater your opportunity to experience the compassion of divine mercy.
3. Stir in your heart a loving complacence at all that Jesus suffered for your sake. Look upon Him on the Cross and see there not just a symbol but the painful reality of His real afflictions. Notice the silence with which Jesus endures so many insults and injuries. Know that His willingness to embrace suffering comes from the compassion His Sacred Heart has for you.

Salesian Devotion

Realizing that love draws the beloved into the lover's heart and the compassion of the Sacred Heart draws us closer to God's own Heart, we can set out each day with greater devotion as we make the long trek around the lake of life toward Jesus.

Behold This Heart

Resolutions

1. On a *personal* level, what might you do to let the Lord cure your ills? Perhaps you can first admit to Him your need for healing, whether physical or emotional or spiritual. Then you might commend to Him your sense of powerlessness or feelings of fear. Finally, you could recognize, in humility and with gratitude, that Jesus suffered willingly and deeply for you.

2. On a *relational* level, what might you do to look upon others with compassion in your heart? Perhaps you could focus on finding something good in those you dislike. You might speak up with a kind word about someone being maligned by others. You could pray to the Sacred Heart for the good of those who have not shown good to you.

3. On a *societal* level, what might you do to alleviate the suffering of the poor and the hungry? Perhaps you could share some of your surplus to help others in need. You might routinely sacrifice a meal you would ordinarily have and donate the money saved to a food bank. Perhaps you could volunteer, individually or as a family, to work with a local human services organization.

Recollections

1. In adoration before the Lord, give thanks for the many ways in which you have benefited from the compassion of others.

2. Remember the inspirations you received from this meditation by calling to mind that *having compassion* can work miracles when disciples of the Lord share with others what little they have.

3. Recall throughout the day this Salesian maxim: "Humility makes our hearts gentle toward the perfect and the imperfect: toward the perfect, out of respect; toward the imperfect, out of compassion" (*Letters of Spiritual Direction*, 121).

MEDITATION 4

The Encouraging Heart of Jesus

ON THE REMEDY FOR FEAR

Our narrative exposition of the Sacred Heart of Jesus continues with the tale of a miraculous encounter between Jesus and His disciples. In this Gospel story, we hear a recurring theme that the Sacred Heart continues to reveal to our world.

JESUS WALKING ON THE SEA OF GALILEE,
BY PAUL BRILL (1590s)

Mark 6:46–52

And after he had taken leave of them, he went up on the mountain to pray. And when evening came, the boat was out on the sea, and he was alone on the land. And he saw that they were making headway painfully, for the wind was against them. And about the fourth watch of the night he came to them, walking on the sea. He meant to pass them by, but when they saw him walking on the sea, they thought it was a ghost, and cried out, for they all saw him and were terrified. But immediately he spoke to them and said, "Take heart, it is I. Do not be afraid." And he got into the boat with them, and the wind ceased. And they were utterly astounded, for they did not understand about the loaves, but their hearts were hardened.

Biblical Narration

It has been a long day! Having fed the multitude, Jesus sends His disciples off ahead of Him, lest they get caught up in the revolutionary fervor of the crowds in Galilee. Meanwhile, He steals away for some solitude and a chance to pray about all that is inevitably weighing on Him.

The time passes quickly. In the last light of *evening*, with the darkness encroaching upon everything, Jesus notices something—the *boat on the sea* with His disciples in it. The *wind* has kicked up. As experienced fishermen, they must have been accustomed to bad weather. Yet this storm proves to be particularly adverse. They strain with *painful* exertion to row the oars in a quest to reach the shore. Yet, despite their best efforts, they make little progress. Clearly, they are in trouble. But He stands far off, *alone on the land.*

Then it happens. Taking the initiative, Jesus moves toward the boat during the *fourth watch*, which is very early in the morning. With the divine power that belongs uniquely to Him, Jesus goes *walking on* the waters of *the sea*. With a supernaturally striking effect, He makes Himself visible to His disciples in the dawning of a new day. He who saw them in trouble draws near, so that they may see His concern for them, the same concern He had shown for others in need the day before.

Yet He *means to pass them by.* Why? Where is He going?

But before He walks any farther, *they all see Him,* though in their confusion, they initially believe they are looking at a ghost. Not surprisingly, they are *terrified.* Is someone really walking on the water? Is it really Jesus? In their perplexity, they can only *cry out* in fear.

Then they hear the words so oft repeated by their Master, a favored utterance meant to change their plight: *"Take heart, it is I. Do not be afraid."* Then He joins them on the boat, and the storm *ceases.* They are safe, at least for now.

"Take Heart"

In the midst of any sort of troubles, Jesus exhorts His followers to "take heart." More than a pleasant wish for good cheer, the expression (from the Greek θαρσέω) calls for a daring choice amid circumstances beyond one's control. It requires the boldness of belief. It necessitates seeing things in a new light.

In divinely dramatic fashion, Jesus shifts the focus of concern from the troubles His disciples face to Himself. He encourages them not to be afraid. Owing to His salvific presence, He invites them to think and feel differently, to have the courage that conquers fear.

With this invitation, Jesus encourages people in a variety of difficult circumstances. Elsewhere in the Gospel story, He sees a paralyzed man, in a culture which considered sin to be at the root of physical illnesses, and says, "Take heart, my son; your sins are forgiven" (Matt. 9:2). He encounters a woman suffering from hemorrhages that have haunted her for more than a decade, and says, "Take heart, daughter; your faith has made you well" (Matt. 9:20). He recognizes in His own disciples a silent consternation at the prospect of their being left alone in a hostile world once

He departs, and says, "Take heart; I have overcome the world" (John 16:33).

If those with Jesus take heart, their plight will change. If they recognize His presence and see how His Heart yearns for their well-being, they can face their fears, their sins, their sufferings, their concerns. If they take heart—*take His Heart*—they can have the courage to overcome their troubles, the courage to live in peace no matter what.

Salesian Spirituality

Anxiety, fear, despair—we inevitably contend with all these at some point during this frail human life. These human realities also figure prominently in our spiritual lives, as the Salesian tradition acknowledges.

From a young age, St. Francis de Sales knew these painful aspects of life. In fact, one such experience would prove to be defining, both for the saint and for the formulation of his thoroughly optimistic spirituality.

While a student in Paris, the young Francis experienced a profound spiritual crisis when his personal devotion and his formal education collided. Listening to university lectures about predestination, he was overwhelmed by the theological dilemma of God's foreknowledge concerning man's salvation; in fact, he took it quite personally. For a six-week period in 1586, he became fixated on the idea that he would be forever damned. He suffered great anguish, in a personal "crisis" brought on by the confluence of physical fatigue, intellectual consternation, and psychological anxiety. Eventually, with fervent prayers to the Blessed Virgin, *Notre Dame de Bonne Délivrance*, he "took heart" and made a prayerful act of abandonment to the divine will. Doing so, he experienced a complete release from his troubles. From this encounter with grace, he learned in his heart and soul not to be afraid; instead, he would always hold on to hope, his courage forever to be based on the merciful presence of God rather than on his own accomplishments.[72]

Based on that formative experience, the future Doctor of the Church would advise others about the dangers of worrying and of the sorrow that derives from it. The former, he notes, "is not a simple temptation but a source from which and by which many temptations arise." In fact, he claims, anxiety "is the greatest evil that can happen to a soul" because "if our heart is inwardly troubled and disturbed it loses both the strength necessary to maintain the virtues it had acquired and the means to resist the temptations of the enemy." With a familiar image, he explains how we ought to proceed:

> Birds stay caught in nets and traps because when they find themselves ensnared they flutter about wildly trying to escape and in so doing entangle themselves all the more. Whenever you urgently desire to escape from a certain evil or to obtain a certain good you must be especially careful both to put your mind at rest and in peace and to have a calm judgment and will. Then try gently and meekly to accomplish your desire, taking in regular order the most convenient means. (*Introduction*, 4:11)

Sadness accompanies anxiety as the result of experiencing the evil we feared; in turn, it becomes the cause of future worries. St. Francis de Sales paints the painful picture of this emotion when he writes that sorrow "disturbs and upsets the soul, arouses inordinate fears, creates disgust for prayer, stupefies and oppresses the brain, deprives the mind of prudence, resolution, judgment, and

---

[72] Dailey, *Live Today Well*, 15.

courage, and destroys its strength." Among the ways to combat anxiety and sadness, the saint suggests prayer—"a sovereign remedy for it lifts up the soul to God who is our only joy and consolation" (*Introduction*, 4:12).

Prayerful Inspiration

St. Francis de Sales counsels courageous and vigorous opposition to these natural tendencies to worry. But how? As it did for him, so for us will the strength for such steadfast courage come through supernatural grace, which remains ever present to us in the Sacred Heart of Jesus. In prayer to Him, we can learn how to "take heart" and be not afraid.

Considerations

1. Reflect on the condition of the world in which we live—and the winds of contradiction swirling all around. Attending to a constant stream of negative news, we struggle to make sense of and find meaning in life. Facing belligerent opposition or hurtful indifference, we strain to see the good in others. Amid reports of violent crime or malicious mayhem, we dwell in apprehension about the future. Created for society, we seem destined to conflict. Desiring peace, we appear to lack solidarity. Through it all, our hearts grow tense.

2. Reflect on your own health—and the emotional or physical sufferings you have to deal with every day. Some come from without, as when we are forced to endure the contempt of others. Some affect us from within, as when we feel sadness or discontent. Some aches are a continual annoyance. Others go deeper and serve as a chronic source of pain. Created for happiness, we long to be freed from this daily grind and

to enjoy a better life. Yet, in that very longing, our hearts become weakened and disturbed.

3. Reflect on the health of your soul—and the sinfulness that impedes your spiritual well-being. Some bad habits we just cannot seem to give up. Some wrongs we are all too quick to commit. With humility we acknowledge that we do what we know we should not, and do not act as we know we should. Created for holiness, we struggle mightily, as if rowing against the secular tide. Failing to be or to do good, our hearts can lose hope.

Affections

1. Arouse in your heart a holy fear. Realize that the agitation brought on by our conflicts, our sufferings, and our sins risks separating us from the God who is the ultimate source of our goodness and our happiness. Like the disciples alone in the boat on the windswept sea, we are powerless on our own to make headway against so many adversities. Yet the Master is nearby.

2. Allow your heart to be consoled. See Jesus coming toward you, the Lord who notices all that you suffer and takes the initiative to save you, just as He has saved the whole world. Envision the power of God at work in the heart that He created within you. Hear His voice and take to heart His words: "It is I. Have faith. I have conquered the world. Do not be afraid."

3. Stir your heart to a supernatural confidence. Be encouraged by the divine presence and the love flowing from the Sacred Heart of Jesus. Realize the truth of what St. Francis de Sales taught to the Visitation Sisters, namely, that humility about our own insufficiencies should beget courage, because "the

greater our knowledge of our own misery, the more profound will be our confidence in the goodness and mercy of God" who provides for our every need. In the Sacred Heart we find the root and source of unfailing courage, for even when we do not feel confident, we can look to Him and see in God's Heart a love for us that never changes (*Spiritual Conferences*, 16–19).

Salesian Devotion

Having been touched by the encouraging Heart of Jesus, and realizing that inspiration finds its completion in action, consider what you might do to practice the devout life today.

Resolutions

1. On a *personal* level, what might you do to attune yourself to the saving presence of Jesus who is ever walking toward you? Knowing your everyday struggles, you could make an act of abandonment to the divine will, with words of prayer that express your faith in God's Providence and mercy. You might learn to take what you cannot control and "offer it up." Perhaps you could choose to go, once again, to receive the Sacrament of Reconciliation.

2. On a *relational* level, what might you do to be a person of encouragement to your family and friends? Perhaps you could reach out to someone you have not seen in a while and spend some of your precious time simply being in his or her company. Perhaps you could be more positive and optimistic when talking to someone who could use a boost to his or her confidence.

3. On a *societal* level, what might you do to spread some hope to a world that needs it? Perhaps you could strive to be more

positive in your social media communications, purposefully injecting optimism where there is so much pessimism. Perhaps you could find a way to help the materially destitute and downtrodden, or to assist those who suffer with mental and emotional distress.

Recollections

1. In adoration before the Lord, give thanks for the gift of His presence and the encouragement of His Sacred Heart.
2. Remember the inspirations you received in this meditation by calling to mind the image of Jesus walking toward you and with you. Pause to hear Him say to you again, *"Take heart."*
3. Recall throughout the day this Salesian maxim: "Walk joyously and open-heartedly as far as you can, and if you do not walk joyously, at least walk courageously and faithfully" (*Letters to Persons in Religion*, 25).

The Broken Heart of Jesus
ON THE WOUND OF LOVE

✛

*In our continuing narrative exposition of the Sacred
Heart, we turn now toward the Passion of the
Christ. We see, first, how even a Sacred Heart can
be hurt – precisely because it loves so much.*

JESUS WEPT, BY JAMES TISSOT (CA. 1886–1894)

John 11:32–37

Now when Mary came where Jesus was and saw him, she fell
at his feet, saying to him, "Lord, if you had been here, my
brother would not have died." When Jesus saw her weeping,
and the Jews who had come with her also weeping, he was
deeply moved in his spirit and greatly troubled. And he said,
"Where have you laid him?" They said to him, "Lord, come
and see." Jesus wept. So the Jews said, "See how he loved
him!" But some of them said, "Could not he who opened the
eyes of the blind man also have kept this man from dying?"

Behold This Heart

Luke 19:41-44

And when he drew near and saw the city, he wept over it, saying, "Would that you, even you, had known on this day the things that make for peace! But now they are hidden from your eyes. For the days will come upon you, when your enemies will set up a barricade around you and surround you and hem you in on every side and tear you down to the ground, you and your children within you. And they will not leave one stone upon another in you, because you did not know the time of your visitation."

Biblical Narration

Once again, Jesus is on the move, this time heading toward the culmination of His public ministry in Jerusalem. His compassionate deeds and encouraging words have made a mark, positively in drawing followers, negatively in attracting the ire of the religious authorities. Despite the objections of those closest to Him, and knowing full well that He is marching toward His death, He remains resolute in His determination to fulfill His mission.

Along the way, though, He receives troubling news: His dear friend, Lazarus, has died (John 11:1-16). Despite the risks, He decides to return to nearby Bethany. No doubt He wants to pay His respects to the mourning family. But even this customary visit will be part of His mission of redemption, for by His words and deeds there, He intends to make known again the glory of God, that His disciples and the crowds may believe.

Upon His arrival, Jesus first encounters Martha, one of the two sisters of Lazarus (John 11:17-27). He announces to her that He is "the resurrection and the life." Martha understands, at least somewhat, and confesses her faith in Him as "the Christ, the Son of God, who is coming into the world."

Then Jesus encounters Mary. Reminiscent of a previous visit (Luke 10:38-42), she again places herself *at His feet* and recognizes Him as *Lord*. But this time she is in tears, *weeping* for her loss. And this time she speaks, uttering the same thought as her sister that this death could have, perhaps should have, been prevented—if only He had been there with them.

The sisters' regret pains their beloved friend. Touched by their tears, He is *deeply moved;* with understandable human emotion, *His* own *spirit* is affected by their loss. Even more, their sadness, and the wailing of all those present, *greatly trouble* Him. Do Martha and Mary think that He has abandoned them? Is the mourning crowd shrieking from genuine sorrow or just making a fuss without any faith?

As in earlier situations, Jesus is again struck deep within by compassion. This time, His misery of heart becomes visible. *Jesus weeps.* Sharing in the human emotion appropriate to the situation, His weeping nevertheless differs in kind; more than mortal sorrow, far from faithless hysteria, Jesus' tears reveal the depth of divine concern for human well-being. He will confirm that supernatural compassion by raising Lazarus from the dead.

The same compassion that figuratively broke Jesus' Heart in Bethany shows itself anew upon the resumption of His journey to Jerusalem. Once again, vociferous crowds have gathered, this time to honor Him with a triumphal entry into the holy city (Luke 19:28-40). They have seen the mighty works Jesus performed along the way; perhaps they witnessed, or at least heard about, the raising of Lazarus. With joyous shouts, they heap praise upon Him, blessing Him as the one "who comes in the name of the Lord."

But Jesus sees *the city* differently. He hears their exultation but reacts with lament. The people there still do not understand *the things that make for peace.* They praise Jesus' might, but fail to see

Him as the Messiah *come in their time.* They rejoice at the possibility of a new life, but its transcendent source remains *hidden from their eyes,* for they fail to recognize the *visitation* of the Son of God in their midst. Intent on political rebellion, their ignorance will lead only to pain and suffering when their holy city is *torn down* to the ground.

Saddened at the sight of such fallen faith, knowing what could have been had this people believed, and perhaps disappointed that His mission has not borne immediate fruit for them, Jesus' Heart is broken. Again, *He weeps.*

"Jesus Wept"

That simple statement—the shortest verse in the Bible in English—expresses most poignantly the affection of the Sacred Heart. Not merely a silent cry, the tears that *Jesus weeps* (from the Greek κλαίω) sound a loud lament. He noticeably sobs for a deceased friend. He wails over a city that has failed to recognize the divine visitation.

The intensity of such mourning escapes narrative description. But its tearful expression matches the deep solicitude God has for people. As a result, when the human-divine Heart is broken by sadness or sorrow, Jesus weeps.

Salesian Spirituality

Tears express heartfelt affection, especially at times of death. No one is immune from them, not even the holy ones of God. St. Francis de Sales wept, as did St. Jane de Chantal, as they freely admit in their letters.[73]

---

[73] See *Selected Letters,* 140–144, in which Francis writes to Jane about the death of his sister, and *Letters of Spiritual Direction,* 206–207, in which Jane writes to her brother about the death of her daughter-in-law.

In the Salesian worldview of a universe of interconnected hearts, tears witness to the bonds of love that already unite us here below and those to which we are oriented eternally.

To be human meant in the Salesian world to have a deep interest in all that is human—especially in the affections, in people's hearts. Whatever is deeply personal and most heartfelt is the stuff of Salesian spirituality. To become fully human one plumbs the resources that one has been given, one searches through the deepest loves of one's heart. There one finds affirmed the fact that there is a correspondence and a similarity of the human and divine realities.[74]

That correspondence of affections finds its ultimate expression in the Sacred Heart of Jesus. Fully human and fully divine, His Heart experiences the misery that necessarily attends true love. St. Francis de Sales points to this truth by noting Jesus' commiseration at seeing the tomb of Lazarus and looking out over the lost city of Jerusalem (*Treatise*, 5:4). With a broken Heart, Jesus weeps.

St. Francis de Sales explains the phenomenon of a broken heart in terms of "the wound of love" experienced in relation to prayer (*Treatise*, 6:13–15). Love first causes pain, he writes, because it draws us out of ourselves toward the good of another. In this respect, love divides our heart by separating us from our self-centeredness; the heart in love, we might say, is cracked open. Love then leads to heartbreak when we realize that the desire aroused in us to make the goodness of the beloved grow cannot be fully satisfied. In this sense, love really is bittersweet: sweet in the heart's profound and affectionate desire, bitter at its powerlessness ever to love enough.

[74] From the editors' introduction in *Letters of Spiritual Direction*, 38–39.

This wound of love is what Jesus experiences and expresses through His eyes. His affection for Martha and Mary leads to tears when He senses their disappointment at His absence and their implicit loss of faith. His desire to bring salvation to God's people turns to weeping over the city when He realizes that they do not apprehend the divine visitation He is making in their midst. The people's failure to accept fully His words and deeds will soon lead to their rejection of Him amid cries to crucify Him.

We, too, experience the wound of love in multiple ways. According to St. Francis de Sales, it happens primarily when we look to the Sacred Heart, for "when we see the Savior of our souls wounded with love for us ... how could we remain unwounded for his sake? But wounded, I say, with a wound so much more painfully loving as his wound was lovingly painful, and I say that we can never love him as much as his love and death demand" (*Treatise*, 6:14). So too our hearts are wounded with love when we remember, as did St. Augustine, that our love for God has been late in coming due to our sinfulness, or when, as St. Margaret Mary did, we think of our indifference to, or willful rejection of, the love of God.

Still, Salesian spirituality favors an optimistic humanism, founded on divine grace. As such, the tears that flow from the wound of love need not be in vain, provided that we humbly place our hearts in the Sacred Heart and firmly put our trust in divine Providence, which willed even the death of the Lord for love of us (*Oeuvres*, 21:36–37).

Prayerful Inspiration

St. Francis de Sales reminds us that the "tears that fall from our eyes are proofs of love" (*Oeuvres*, 10:13). We see this when Jesus wept. We know it when we cry. In meditation upon the wound of love in the Sacred Heart, we can plumb the depths of this divine and human reality.

Considerations

1. Reflect on the tears you see shed on a daily basis throughout the world. We hear mothers wailing over their children who died as a result of gun violence. We see the pain on the faces of those whose loved ones were taken from them as the result of injustice. Such needless suffering. Such disregard for human life and indifference to human dignity. So many broken hearts.

2. Inquire into the state of your own heart, especially with regard to those you love. Recall the times you have cried for them, with a heart wounded by love. See how your concern for others inevitably leads to suffering, precisely because you can never love them enough.

3. Ponder the state of your soul with regard to your love of God. Remember those times that you were indifferent to God's love for you or those opportunities when you failed to return love for love. Reflect upon the fact that "life past is a thing of horror to life present for one who has passed his preceding life without loving the supreme good" (*Treatise*, 6:14).

Affections

1. Arouse in yourself a sense of condolence for the broken hearts of others. Experience how real their pain is by imagining yourself in their situation. Bring to your heart a greater appreciation of the fact that as we share in human life, so we share in human dignity, which leads us also to share in human suffering.

2. Stir your heart to tears—not in pain but in love. Taste the sweetness of your concern for family and friends. Feel the bitterness of not being able to care for them enough. Rouse the desire to love them even more.

3. Humble your heart by looking to the wounds of the Sacred Heart of Jesus. Acknowledge that you are unworthy of the depths of such divine compassion. Be remorseful for any indifference you have shown to His love for you. Be vulnerable before Him—allowing yourself to be loved by Him rather than focusing on what you could or should do for Him. See in His broken Heart and tortured body the extent to which God desires to share His merciful consolation with you.

Salesian Devotion

Recognizing that God "wants our misery to be the throne of His mercy, and our powerlessness the seat of His omnipotence" (*Thy Will Be Done*, 142), let us endeavor to live the devout life amid the tears we inevitably experience.

Resolutions

1. On a *personal* level, what might you do to address the wounds in your heart? Perhaps you could bring yourself to forgive someone who has failed you. Or you might try to reconcile with a family member with whom you have been separated. Perhaps you could simply visit a long-lost relative or friend.

2. On a *relational* level, what might you do to help others whose hearts are broken? Perhaps you could commiserate with a neighbor who recently lost a loved one. Or you might have Masses offered for someone you know who has died. Perhaps

you could even start or assist with a bereavement group at your parish or in your community.

3. On a *societal* level, what might you do to advance a greater love for life in a world increasingly indifferent to human dignity? Perhaps you could join a pro-life organization. Or you might volunteer your time to assist people with mental or physical challenges. Perhaps you could serve at a local nursing home or eldercare facility.

Recollections

1. In adoration before the Lord, give thanks for those persons in your life who love you to tears.

2. Remember the inspirations you received in this meditation by calling to mind the image of *Jesus weeping* out of love for you.

3. Recall throughout the day this Salesian maxim: "In love there is no pain, or if there is pain, it is well-loved pain" (*Treatise*, 6:14).

The Abiding Heart of Jesus
ON THE ENDURANCE OF LOVE

✠

Our narrative exposition of the Sacred Heart of Jesus
continues toward the Passion of the Christ as we
hear some of the Master's parting instructions to His
disciples. In this passage, we are invited to attend
to the divine presence at the heart of the gospel.

CHRIST TEACHING THE TWELVE APOSTLES
(EARLY FIFTEENTH CENTURY)

John 15:9–17

As the Father has loved me, so have I loved you. Abide in
my love. If you keep my commandments, you will abide
in my love, just as I have kept my Father's commandments
and abide in his love. These things I have spoken to you,
that my joy may be in you, and that your joy may be full.
This is my commandment, that you love one another as
I have loved you. Greater love has no one than this, that

someone lay down his life for his friends. You are my friends if you do what I command you. No longer do I call you servants, for the servant does not know what his master is doing; but I have called you friends, for all that I have heard from my Father I have made known to you. You did not choose me, but I chose you and appointed you that you should go and bear fruit and that your fruit should abide, so that whatever you ask the Father in my name, he may give it to you. These things I command you, so that you will love one another.

Biblical Narration

After the tearful detour to Bethany, Jesus enters the holy city of Jerusalem. Joyous acclamations accompany Him, but He knows that the hour of His suffering and death is drawing near. Before that hour arrives, and away from the misguided crowds, He takes the opportunity to provide His apostles with a few final lessons, the thrust of which He will enact in the coming week.

Prior to His "farewell discourse" (John 14–17), Jesus washes the feet of the apostles, performing for them the fundamental action He asks of every disciple, namely, that they treat others as more important to them than they are to themselves. He warns His companions of His forthcoming betrayal and foretells their denial. At the same time, He declares that He will not abandon them but will, instead, send the Spirit of Truth to help them.

Perhaps perplexed by the seemingly conflicting messages, and probably overwhelmed by the finality of their Master's words, the apostles must have been growing distraught. They made it this far with Him, but the next steps in their discipleship appear risky at best and futile at worst. Will they emerge unscathed from the forces of violent opposition marshalling all around them? Can they survive on their own without the wisdom and power of the One who has brought them this far?

Jesus seems to sense their interior struggle as He prepares for His own. Recognizing the stressful situation, He seeks in this farewell discourse to assure them that they are not alone. From the heart He speaks with affection the words that embrace the whole of their shared journey: "*As the Father has loved me, so have I loved you.*"

There. He has said it. And that says it all.

The apostles understand the premise to be true, for they have heard the voice from the heavens say so. Considering the encouraging words and compassionate deeds they have witnessed during their time with Jesus, they could also assume the truth of the conclusion. But hearing Him say it—so plainly, so clearly, so directly—they now know unmistakably what regard He has for them. In those words—"*As the Father has loved me, so have I loved you*"—they experience the Sacred Heart speaking to them.

But beyond sharing a sentiment or stating a fact, as profound as that is, the Master also extends an invitation to them—to remain there, to dwell in that divine love. As a vine is connected to its branches, so the hearts of Jesus and His apostles are now intertwined. He is the vine; they are the branches (see John 15:5). He who is eternally united with the Father has *made known* God's Word to them. Now He promises to *abide* in them, to remain present to them and with them and for them, to be the vital source of the rest of their lives.

In turn, He bids them to *abide in His love.* When they do so—they who have been *chosen* and *appointed* and are now called "*friends*"—they will bear the good fruit of living in *love* for *one another.* And by their living of this new commandment, people will come to know the One whose disciples they are.

Behold This Heart

"Abiding" in Love

Frequently repeated in this chapter of John's Gospel, the notion of "*abiding*" (from the Greek μένω) conveys a sense of permanent dwelling. More than simply a reference to time or place, the term evokes a sense of expectancy in the context of a relationship that endures.

Those who have followed Jesus so closely in the journey toward the kingdom can now be confident that He will not abandon them. Though He departs from them, Jesus nevertheless remains with them. The love of the Lord for them continues, just as the Father's love for the Beloved Son abides eternally.

That, in summary, is the gospel message—not only for the apostles but for all who follow Christ. Jesus remains with us; His divine presence is not somewhere else, distant from us. Abiding with us, He continues to assure us of His friendship. When our hearts remain connected to the Lord's, then His *joy* will *be in* us. When we remain aware of how He has loved us, then our *joy* will *be full*. And when we return love for love, then our lives will be complete. The Sacred Heart assures us of this.

Salesian Spirituality

The Salesian tradition encourages discernment of God's abiding presence everywhere, including in the works of creation, the operation of the Church, and the grace of the sacraments. By the power of the Holy Spirit, the same Paraclete that Jesus promised to send to His apostles, God remains present also within us through His "inspirations." St. Francis de Sales describes these as "all those interior attractions, motions, acts of self-reproach and remorse, lights, and conceptions that God works in us and predisposes our hearts by his blessing, fatherly care, and love in order to awaken, stimulate, urge, and attract us to holy virtues, heavenly love, and good resolutions, in short, to everything that sends us on our way to everlasting welfare" (*Introduction*, 2:18).

As we make that journey to eternal life, the saint counsels us, we should conduct our daily lives according to the dual dynamic of devotion, namely, paying attention and directing our intention. The former seeks a deepening awareness of God's presence in our lives, which can happen through moments of recollection or "spiritual retreat" in which we pause from the busyness of our lives to consider how God remains with us. "Indeed," St. Francis de Sales notes, "our tasks are seldom so important as to keep us from withdrawing our hearts from them from time to time in order to retire into this divine solitude" (*Introduction*, 2:12). The busy bishop of Geneva lived by his own words, almost continuously dwelling in a recollected state, as St. Jane de Chantal attests: "I once asked him whether he ever went for any length of time without actually and explicitly turning his mind to God, and he said: 'Sometimes for as long as about a quarter of an hour'" (*Testimony*, 97).

But, like the apostles and all the saints, we must practice the "new commandment" of loving one another in all things to abide in the divine presence. To this end, St. Francis de Sales proposes that we use our minds and hearts and wills to direct our intention to God in all that we do. Specifically, he advises that

> if we wish to thrive and advance in the way of our Lord, we should, at the beginning of our actions, both exterior and interior, ask for his grace and offer to his divine Goodness all the good we will do. In this way we will be prepared to bear with peace and serenity all the pain and suffering we will encounter as coming from the fatherly hand of our good God and Savior. His most holy intention is to have

us merit by such means in order to reward us afterward out of the abundance of his love.[75]

Drawing upon our awareness of Jesus' love dwelling within us and among us, we can strive to return love for love by intentionally doing whatever we do for God's sake. Then we, too, shall abide in His love.

Prayerful Inspiration

St. Jane de Chantal reminds us of St. Francis de Sales's conviction that "the best possible prayer [is] to fall in love with our Lord's will and accept it whole-heartedly" (*Testimony*, 96). This we can do through a meditative awareness of the Sacred Heart and its grace in our lives.

Considerations

1. Reflect upon the world in all its created splendor. Marvel at the magnificence, the complexity, and the order of nature. Ponder how the guiding hand of our Creator makes it all possible, despite some popular worldviews that deny the work of a divine master craftsman. Acknowledge where and how God remains present in the world, despite claims to the contrary made by an increasingly secular culture.

2. Reflect, also, on your own place in this world. Realize that God has created you to be in this specific moment in history, that He has chosen and appointed you for this particular life, and that without you, the world would be a very different place. Acknowledge that your continued existence is a daily gift.

---

[75] From St. Francis de Sales's *Spiritual Directory*, cited and more fully explained in chapter 5 of Dailey, *Live Today Well*.

3. Withdraw into your soul to consider how the divine Spirit "breathes" you into life this very day and sustains you every day. Examine whether there is more room for God to abide there. Acknowledge the ways in which you inhibit Him from doing so.

Affections

1. Arouse in yourself a sense of gratitude for the life you have and are called to live. Be thankful for the supernatural grace that keeps you in existence. Be receptive to the divine inspirations that send you on your way toward eternal well-being. Let yourself be moved by the awareness that with each passing hour of each passing day, you are drawing nearer to eternity.

2. Humble yourself for the times when you have failed to see the presence of God in the people you have encountered, the places you have gone, or the things you have done. Stir yourself to regret for having missed any opportunities to rest or dwell in God's presence. Rouse yourself to the desire to seek and find Him wherever He abides.

3. Embrace the peace that God offers you in the midst of this troubling world through the sacraments you have received. Delight in the Word you have heard Him speak to you at Mass. Relish the opportunity to receive Him within you in the Eucharist. Stir yourself to adore and worship Him who has loved you and remains always present to and for you.

Salesian Devotion

Attentive to God's presence, and realizing that "it is not by the multiplicity of things we do that we acquire perfection, but by the perfection and purity of intention with which we do them" (*Spiritual Conferences*, 238), let us endeavor to love one another in whatever we do so as to abide in God's love.

Resolutions

1. On a *personal* level, what might you do to be more aware of, and accepting of, the abiding presence of Jesus in your own life? Perhaps you could intentionally pause once in a while to take a deep breath and recognize that the Spirit of God is alive in you, even in the midst of your struggles. Or you might speak to yourself a holy thought with each passing hour of the day. Or you could try practicing a direction of intention before a particular task you have each day.

2. On a *relational* level, what might you do to see how God dwells in the lives of those you often encounter? With co-workers, perhaps you could greet them first with a kind word or friendly smile. With neighbors, you might praise them for something they accomplished or thank them anew for something they have done for you. With family members, you might try to follow their preference when it comes to some activity you are considering.

3. On a *societal* level, what might you do to foster awareness of God's presence in all people? Perhaps you could do something to feed the poor, clothe the naked, shelter the stranger, care for the sick, or visit the imprisoned, as Jesus bids us to do for the least of His people (Matt. 25:31–46). Or you might work to mitigate discrimination in your workplace and in society. Or you could pray more earnestly for an end to unjust oppression and violence in our world.

Recollections

1. In adoration before the Lord, give thanks for the gift of Jesus' *abiding* presence with us in the Blessed Sacrament.

2. Remember the inspirations you received in this meditation by calling to mind the words Jesus addressed to the apostles and now speaks to you: "*As the Father has loved me, so have I loved you.*"

3. Recall throughout the day this Salesian maxim concerning Holy Communion: "You cannot consider our Savior in an action more full of love or more tender than this. In it he abases himself, if we may so express it, and changes himself into food, so that he may penetrate our souls and unite himself most intimately to the heart and body of his faithful" (*Introduction*, 2:21).

The Troubled Heart of Jesus

ON THE PASSION BETWEEN LOVE AND DEATH

☩

Our narrative exposition now enters into the Passion of Christ and the fullest revelation of the Sacred Heart. It begins in the Garden of Gethsemane, where we witness the anguish that links love and death in Jesus' obedience to the will of His Father.

CHRIST IN THE GARDEN OF GETHSEMANE, *BY LUCAS CRANACH THE ELDER (CA. 1540)*

Mark 14:32–42

And they went to a place called Gethsemane. And he said to his disciples, "Sit here while I pray." And he took with him Peter and James and John, and began to be greatly distressed and troubled. And he said to them, "My soul is

very sorrowful, even to death. Remain here and watch."
And going a little farther, he fell on the ground and prayed
that, if it were possible, the hour might pass from him.
And he said, "Abba, Father, all things are possible for you.
Remove this cup from me. Yet not what I will, but what
you will." And he came and found them sleeping, and
he said to Peter, "Simon, are you asleep? Could you not
watch one hour? Watch and pray that you may not enter
into temptation. The spirit indeed is willing, but the flesh
is weak." And again he went away and prayed, saying the
same words. And again he came and found them sleeping,
for their eyes were very heavy, and they did not know what
to answer him. And he came the third time and said to
them, "Are you still sleeping and taking your rest? It is
enough; the hour has come. The Son of Man is betrayed
into the hands of sinners. Rise, let us be going; see, my
betrayer is at hand."

Biblical Narration

The troubles begin.

What the Master foretold and His apostles feared has come
upon them. Despite assurances to the contrary, He will be taken
from them; more to the point, He will give Himself—His Heart
and His life—for them.

First, Jesus and the apostles go together to a garden called *Gethsemane*—an idyllic spot, recalling the environment in which human
life originated; a fruitful locale, where olive trees substitute for the
vines and branches to which Jesus likened their relationship not
long ago; a peaceful place, outside the hectic city where, ordinarily,
solitude could be sought and rest found. But not on this night.

Stealing away from the group with *Peter and James and John*—the same trio who enjoyed the vision and heard the voice on the mountaintop—Jesus becomes *greatly distressed* over what is about to happen. Suffering the dread of anticipation, He is more deeply *troubled* at the finality of what His mission demands of Him.

He acknowledges to these friends the depths of His distress, describing it as a sorrowful feeling, an anguish reaching into His very *soul* and touching upon His mortality. The existential burden weighs so heavily on Him that He cannot bear it alone. But He must. So He separates Himself from them, *going a little farther* away while they *remain* behind.

But Jesus is not alone; He abides in the Father's love. Still, He *falls to the ground*—just as the frightened witnesses did under the bright cloud enveloping the scene of the Transfiguration. Shrouded in eerie darkness rather than dazzling light, this moment also portends fear. But Jesus' experience differs from that of His disciples. He is not scared of death, but *sorrowful to death*—tormented by the realization that His Father's plan for salvation demands this much from Him. Yet, as He had previously admitted, it is for this very purpose that He has come to such a troubling hour (John 12:27-33).

The suffering soon to be inflicted upon Him by the local authorities and their cohorts here afflicts Him interiorly. He *prays* to His heavenly *Father*, tenderly yet earnestly invoking His "*Abba*,"[76] in the hope that another way may be possible. Yes, even His human *flesh* is *weak* at the prospect of dying. But His *willing spirit* breathes in such complete union with God that Jesus accedes to His Father's providential plan.

---

[76] An Aramaic term, used specifically in the direct address of prayer and denoting the familiarity and intimacy of a paternal relationship, not unlike the use of "dad" or "daddy" in English.

Between heaven and earth, the Hearts of Father and Son remain connected. *That is enough.* Though His disciples may not be ready, it is now time to *be going.* *The hour* to redeem humanity *has come.*

"Sorrowful unto Death"

While the impending pains will be savage in their physical brutality, the torment that Jesus suffers while pondering His fate in Gethsemane is no less excruciating. By His own admission, what Jesus anticipates makes Him *sorrowful, even to death.* The intensity of such "grief all around" Him (περίλυπος in Greek) produces within Him a sorrow at once poignant and perplexing, a distress so agonizing as to be almost too much to bear.

In Jesus, existential anguish is generated by, and comes to expression in, His ultimate concern for human beings. In the Sacred Heart, we see how the dual dimensions of divine "passion" — love and suffering — are inextricably connected.

Salesian Spirituality

Central to the Salesian worldview of interconnected hearts is the operation of the will (which is thought to be "located" in the heart). Truly loving hearts take delight in what is good (complacence) and act in ways to make that goodness grow (benevolence).[77] Integrated into a devout life, these two movements exert a reciprocal influence that leads to the fulfillment of the great commandment to love God and neighbor.

As made evident by Jesus' experience in the Garden of Gethsemane, affective love can cause great anguish in one's soul, while effective love can call for the abandonment of one's desires. While

---

[77] St. Francis de Sales explores these "two chief exercises of sacred love" in book 5 of the *Treatise on the Love of God.*

these demands may seem burdensome, St. Francis de Sales believes that they make for progress in perfection. That spiritual journey, he says, requires us to live courageously between two wills of God.[78]

The one is God's "signified will" as it is made known to us by more or less explicit means. For St. Francis de Sales, this includes "the truths which God wills that we should believe, the goods he will have us hope for, the pains he will have us dread, what he will have us love, the commandments he will have us observe, and the counsels he desires us to follow" (*Treatise*, 8:3). We can know this signified will through the words of Sacred Scripture, in what is stated as law (the Commandments) or counseled as wise (for example, the Beatitudes) or promoted as virtuous (such as the evangelical counsels of chastity, poverty, and obedience). We also come to understand it through the explicit teaching of those commissioned by God to teach it (namely, the Church's Magisterium). Finally, we can recognize it in the "laws" reflected in nature. To submit to these various manifestations of God's will—to conform our lives to them—represents one way to love God.

The other aspect of the divine will is God's "good pleasure." For St. Francis de Sales, this summarily refers to all those things that happen to us but are not brought about by us. Whether comforting or afflicting, pleasurable or painful, the daily events that take place in the course of human life show us, by their having happened, that God has willed and intended them (*Treatise*, 9:1). In particular, the saint has in mind those inexplicable ways in which we might suffer due to no fault of our own. To accept distressing trials for the love of God, he says, is the high point of charity, because our human nature inclines us to avoid or reject whatever

---

[78] See *Treatise on the Love of God*, books 8 and 9. The summary that follows is taken from Dailey, *Live Today Well*, 60-61.

pains us. But in the Salesian perspective, the sorrowful things we do not understand or find hard to accept occur within the orbit of divine Providence. And since God wills only what is good for us, even those things that grieve us are ultimately intended for our eternal benefit.

Prayerful Inspiration

St. Francis de Sales reminds us that conforming or submitting to the will of God requires a continual education of the heart, in which we learn "to desire to love and love to desire what can never be enough desired or loved" (*Letters to Persons in the World*, 4). The Sacred Heart of Jesus can teach us this lesson through meditative prayer.

Considerations

1. Think about today's world—with so much evidence of "grief all around." We are daily reminded of racial tensions, abuses of power, and ravages of persecution and war that torment every society. Consider the ways in which you may contribute, directly or indirectly, to these social structures of sin.

2. Reflect upon your own life—in particular, the suffering you endure that you have not caused. That suffering may be physical, entailing chronic or debilitating pain. It may be emotional, fueled by hurts from past relationships or significant worries in the present day.

3. Ponder the state of your own soul—and your willingness to follow God's will in all its manifestations. Ask yourself whether you accept all that the Church teaches about the life of faith and morals. Consider how you receive the surprises,

good and bad, that come with daily life. Acknowledge where you fall short in living courageously between these two wills of God.

Affections

1. Fall before the Lord (figuratively speaking) in humility of heart. Offer to God whatever sorrow you may be experiencing. Gather the courage to ask God about the situations you cannot control and the grace to abandon your wants in favor of God's will.

2. Commiserate with Jesus in Gethsemane. Feel the conflict between His human will to live and His divine mission to die. Empathize, to the extent you can, with having to do something you would prefer not to do. Offer your own dilemmas to the Father and open yourself to His heavenly guidance.

3. Stir in your heart an affection for God as your "Abba"—a loving Father who has protected your life and provided for your needs. Rouse yourself to the desire to embrace whatever your heavenly Father wills for you from this day forward.

Salesian Devotion

In a truly devout prayer life, the affective dimension that cultivates a love of God necessarily leads to an effective dimension that demonstrates a love for God in how we act. Consider how to live that integrated spirituality in your life.

Resolutions

1. On a *personal* level, what might you do to ease the burden of significant decisions you must make? Perhaps you could

dedicate more time for solitude and sacred silence. Or you might decide to look into and follow a specific process of spiritual discernment. Or you could seek out a qualified spiritual director to help guide your life.

2. On a *relational* level, what might you do to "keep watch" with people in sorrowful situations? Perhaps you could check in on neighbors or distant relatives just to see how they are doing, especially if you know them to be struggling in some way. Or you might call upon your personal or professional contacts to help a friend or colleague in need. Or you could pray for others' intentions during a holy hour.[79]

3. On a *societal* level, what might you do to lessen the "grief all around" us? Perhaps you could learn more about the background of people whose culture differs from yours. Or you might participate in efforts to bring together people of different races or religions. Or you could take a look at your financial investments to determine who ultimately benefits from them and decide, where necessary and appropriate, to change who receives your support.

Recollections

1. In adoration before the Lord, give thanks for His willingness to suffer torment to carry out the Father's plan of salvation for you.

2. Remember the inspirations you received in this meditation by calling to mind the image of Jesus praying in Gethsemane,

---

[79] Explained further in the second appendix, this devotional practice issues from St. Margaret Mary's experience (*Life*, 170) and recalls the time Jesus spent in prayer in Gethsemane.

with His Sacred Heart "*sorrowful unto death*" because of His passionate concern for you and for all of humanity.

3. Recall throughout the day this Salesian maxim: "Love's principal power is to enable the lover to suffer for the beloved" (*Treatise*, 9:2).

The Pierced Heart of Jesus
ON THE PRICE PAID FOR
OUR REDEMPTION

✠

*Our narrative exposition now brings us to Calvary, where
the Sacred Heart of Jesus is opened to the world in the
culmination of the Passion. In this dramatic scene, divine
love is poured out for the redemption of humanity.*

CHRIST ON THE CROSS BETWEEN THE TWO
THIEVES, BY PETER PAUL RUBENS (1619–1620)

John 19:33–37

Since it was the day of Preparation, and so that the bodies
would not remain on the cross on the Sabbath (for that
Sabbath was a high day), the Jews asked Pilate that their
legs might be broken and that they might be taken away.
So the soldiers came and broke the legs of the first, and of
the other who had been crucified with him. But when they
came to Jesus and saw that he was already dead, they did

not break his legs. But one of the soldiers pierced his side with a spear, and at once there came out blood and water. He who saw it has borne witness—his testimony is true, and he knows that he is telling the truth—that you also may believe. For these things took place that the Scripture might be fulfilled: "Not one of his bones will be broken." And again another Scripture says, "They will look on him whom they have pierced."

Biblical Narration

The end has come.

The dark night of agony in the garden ends with Jesus' being led out in chains, suspected of fomenting religious rebellion. Shrouded further by the corrupt machinations of religious authorities and political governors, this night turns into a day of cruel and horrifying punishment.

After being tortured and mocked, the innocent prisoner is led on a trek through the streets of the holy city. Under the stress and strain of carrying the Cross, and enduring all manner of public scorn and derision, Jesus eventually reaches the ignominious hill known as "the Skull." There He will be subjected to the brutal vengeance for which Roman soldiers were notorious. He is nailed to the Cross He carried, strung up to die along with two others. Left there for hours, He is unable to move without His limbs being torn by the spikes that fix Him aloft. Suffocating with every breath He struggles to take, He is dehydrated far beyond His admitted thirst.

Still, He knows this is where He is meant to be. Here will be the fulfillment of His life's work. Here will be His moment of victory and exaltation. Here will be the completion of His mission, the ultimate expression of His perfect obedience to the Father's will.

Conclusively uttering "it is finished," He chooses to yield up His spirit. Bowing His head, He breathes forth His last breath and dies.

But the spectacle continues. What happens next reveals the never-ending love of the Sacred Heart.

Not without coincidence, this day of crucifixion was the *day of preparation* of the sacrificial lambs for the Jewish Passover. As this initiates the *high* holy *days* of the Jewish Passover, concerned leaders worry that the optics of the Sabbath will be ruined, believers disturbed and distracted, and religious worship waylaid if the prominent display of worldly (in)justice continues any longer. The executed need to *be taken away*, contrary to the Roman custom of leaving them aloft for all to see.

To hasten death, the soldiers *break the legs* of the crucified, thereby impeding their ability to push themselves up in order to take a breath. But the legs of Jesus do not need to be broken. The soldiers know He is *already dead*; they saw and heard Him yield His spirit of His own volition. Still, they have to ascertain the finality of their cruel work. So *one of the soldiers pierces His side with a spear*, thrusting the lance with military precision toward the most vital human organ in an effort to probe for signs of life.

Those signs appear *at once* in the *blood and water* that *comes out* from the opened wound. Torn by a soldier's spear, but also ruptured by the physical and emotional agonies suffered throughout His Passion, the Sacred Heart of Jesus here offers a conclusive revelation, the very stuff of that Heart disclosing in visible ways the invisible mystery of life and love.

Flowing from Jesus' body, the blood that gives vitality to life and the water that washes clean with compassion reveal the truth of who Jesus is and the price He has paid for our redemption. Henceforth, all who *look on Him* can see not only the agony of what transpired that day on Calvary, but also the superabundance of love that comprises the meaning and significance of the Good Friday event.

Now they who *believe* in that truth can obtain salvation from Him whose Sacred Heart was opened that day. From His wounds grace continues to pour forth in prayer and in the celebration of the sacraments of the Church, which the blood and water symbolize.

"Pierced with a Sword"

For Roman soldiers, the use of a sword was not uncommon. On this day, however, the ordinary becomes extraordinary.

The soldier on Calvary thrusts his spear into the flesh of a condemned man. *Pierced* (from the Greek νύσσω) in this way, the body is wounded openly but not mortally. The wound does not need to be lethal since Jesus has already died. But the lance is sharp enough to cut into the flesh, an incision that proved to be inspiring.

The soldier's pragmatic piercing of the crucified Jesus on that fateful day transfixes the Savior in a permanent way. Not only does it confirm the fact of physical death, but also it affirms the source of spiritual life. From that single thrust of a spear comes the inextinguishable force of the Sacred Heart—and the enduring image of divine compassion and mercy that will inspire believers for ages to come.

Salesian Spirituality

In his detailed study on references to the heart in the writings of St. Francis de Sales, John Abruzzese writes, "If 'love is,' as de Sales insists, 'the abridgement of all theology,' then it can be said that the crucified Christ, and in particular the pierced Heart of Christ, is the abridgement of all Salesian thought on the theology of hearts."[80]

[80] John A. Abruzzese, *The Theology of Hearts in the Writings of St. Francis de Sales* (Rome: Pontifical University of St. Thomas Aquinas, 1983), 149, citing *Treatise*, 8:1.

That theology sees in the crucified Christ the source of life and the origin of love. For St. Francis de Sales, the pulsing Heart of the child in Mary's womb that led John the Baptist to leap for joy in the womb of Elizabeth first points to the new life Jesus brings, "that is to say, a life more perfect and more pleasing to God, a life which will render them [men and women] capable of uniting themselves more closely to divine goodness."[81] The pierced Heart of Jesus on the Cross then purchases that life for humanity, as the saint explains in one of his sermons for Good Friday:

> Our Lord possesses a life that is not common and small, but a *superabundant life* (John 10:10), to the end that every person participates in it and lives from this same life, which is that of grace, entirely perfect and entirely loveable. But for us to acquire this life, Our Lord purchased it for us at the price of his blood and by the lance in his side. Therefore, our life is not ours, but his; we are no longer our own, but his. (*Oeuvres*, 9:269–270)

This purchase of new life by way of Jesus' death leads St. Francis de Sales also to posit the origins of love in that same Sacred Heart. "All love that does not take its origin from the Savior's passion," he writes, "is foolish and perilous. Unhappy is death without the Savior's love; unhappy is love without the Savior's death. Love and death are so intermingled in the Savior's passion that we cannot have the one in our hearts without the other" (*Treatise*, 12:13).

This superabundant life and love are the foundations to the Salesian spirituality of a universe of interconnected hearts. In this worldview, the image of the pierced Heart of Jesus remains central and serves a twofold spiritual purpose. On the one hand, God

---

[81] *Spiritual Conferences*, 92, cited in Abruzzese, *Theology of Hearts*, 143.

looks outward from that pierced Heart to gaze upon the world and those dwelling in it. As the saint writes:

> God's love is seated within the Savior's heart as on a royal throne. He beholds through the cleft of his pierced side all the hearts of the children of men. His heart is king of hearts, and he keeps his eyes fixed on our hearts. Just as those who peer through a lattice see clearly while they themselves are only half seen, so too the divine love within that heart, or rather that heart of divine love, always clearly sees our hearts and looks on them with the eyes of love, while we do not see him, but only half see him. (*Treatise*, 5:11)

On the other hand, looking into that pierced heart is how human beings can see and come to God. In another sermon, St. Francis de Sales explains this capability in terms of divine intentionality:

> Our Lord willed that his side be opened for several reasons. The first is to the end that one would see the thoughts of his heart, which were thoughts of love and dilection for us, his beloved children and dear creatures, that he had created in his image and likeness, to the end that we would see how much he desires to give graces and blessings to us, and his very heart....
>
> The second reason is to the end that we would go to him with complete confidence, to withdraw ourselves and hide within his side, in order to repose in him, seeing that he had opened it to receive us there with an unparalleled graciousness and love, if only we give ourselves to him and abandon ourselves entirely and without reserve to his goodness and providence. (*Oeuvres*, 9:80)

United with God in and through the pierced Heart of Jesus, we are called to a devout life that responds in kind, as the saint preaches in 1622 in another sermon for Good Friday:

> Now, since God's Son was crucified for us, what remains for us at this hour but to crucify with Him our flesh with its passions and desires. For love is repaid with love alone.... By rendering Our Lord love for love and the praises and blessings we owe Him for His Death and Passion, we will be confessing Him as our Liberator and Saviour. (*Sermons for Lent*, 184)

Prayerful Inspiration

Because "nothing urges on a man's heart so much as love," and "we know that Jesus Christ, true God, eternal and almighty, has loved us even so far as to will to suffer death for us," we can learn to repay our Lord's love with our love by living "no more according to human reason and inclinations but above them according to the inspirations and promptings of the divine Savior of our souls" (*Treatise*, 7:8). We learn this lesson through meditation upon the Sacred Heart.

Considerations

1. Reflect upon the condition of the world today, in which people everywhere continue to be "pierced" by human cruelty. All too often, innocent citizens are subject to the ravages of war and the pains of persecution. All too wantonly, governmental powers resort to torture. All too recklessly, global corporations support unjust practices that, for the sake of greed or power, bring pain to the poor.

2. Consider the part you may play in "piercing" the hearts of others: by the angry conversations you have with those at

home, by your impatient reaction to others on the road, by the stabbing words you utter in criticism or gossip or slander, or by your silent indifference to those who suffer.

3. Ponder the state of your own soul in relation to the pierced Heart of Jesus. Examine whether you live more by natural inclinations and desires than by supernatural inspiration and guidance. Consider honestly whether you give the Lord sufficient praise and blessing for having suffered for you in His Passion.

Affections

1. Looking upon the pierced Heart of Jesus, let your heart be filled with sorrow for all the pains He endured as the price paid for your redemption. With a loving condolence, see the emptying of that Sacred Heart as an outpouring of all that He could give for your salvation.

2. Looked at by the pierced Heart of Jesus, rouse yourself to remorse for your sins. Realizing the many ways in which you perpetuate the piercing of that Sacred Heart, humble yourself before the God whose love is enthroned there.

3. Looking into the pierced Heart of Jesus, arouse in yourself a deep gratitude for the unparalleled love shown to you on the Cross. Abandon yourself again to God's goodness and mercy, which flowed from the wounds of His Son's crucified body. Be consoled by the outpouring of grace from that Sacred Heart, in which you can have complete confidence.

Salesian Devotion

Realizing that "we live only because he died," and that "therefore, we must no longer live as belonging to ourselves but to him, not in ourselves but in him, and not for ourselves but for him" (*Treatise*, 7:8), let us endeavor to live devoutly and discern how we can repay love for love.

Resolutions

1. On a *personal* level, what might you do to grow in your appreciation of the Sacred Heart of Jesus? Perhaps you could place an image in your car or enthrone an image in your home where you would routinely see it and be reminded of its meaning. Or you might learn more about the Passion or the Sacred Heart devotion. Or you could make a regular holy hour or participate in First Friday devotions.[82]

2. On a *relational* level, what might you do to help others become aware of the graces of the Sacred Heart? Perhaps you could give your family or friends a gift that would draw their attention to the Sacred Heart. Or you might bring them to visit a chapel or church dedicated to the Sacred Heart. Or you could invite them to join you in devotional prayers to the Sacred Heart.

3. On a *societal* level, what might you do to spread devotion to the Sacred Heart of Jesus? Perhaps you could start a group at your parish to practice devotion to the Sacred Heart. Or you could join a public association dedicated to the Sacred Heart. Or you could offer support to religious congregations inspired by the Sacred Heart.

Recollections

1. In adoration before the Lord, give thanks for the opportunity you have to participate in the Mass, where, in the

---

[82] See the "Promises of the Sacred Heart Given to Margaret Mary Alacoque" in the second appendix of this book.

Eucharist, Christ's body is broken again for you and His blood shed for you.

2. Remember the inspirations you received in this meditation by calling to mind the image of the *pierced Heart* of Jesus and its ever-present outpouring of love upon you and upon the world.

3. Recall throughout the day this Salesian maxim from St. Margaret Mary: "Even the most bitter sufferings are sweet in this adorable Heart, where everything is changed into love."[83]

---

[83] *Letters of St. Margaret Mary Alacoque*, 5.

The Living Heart of Jesus
ON FAITH IN THE RESURRECTION

✛

Having reached its culmination in the Crucifixion,
our narrative exposition now considers the lasting
impact of the revelation of the Sacred Heart. In His
post-Resurrection appearance to Thomas and the other
apostles, Jesus links faith to "seeing" His living Heart.

THE INCREDULITY OF THOMAS,
BY MAERTEN DE VOS (1574)

John 20:19–20, 24–29

On the evening of that day, the first day of the week, the doors being locked where the disciples were for fear of the Jews, Jesus came and stood among them and said to them, "Peace be with you." When he had said this, he showed them his hands and his side. Then the disciples were glad when they saw the Lord.... Now Thomas, one of the twelve, called the Twin, was not with them when Jesus came. So the other disciples told him, "We have seen the Lord." But he said to them, "Unless I see in his hands the mark of the nails, and place my finger into the mark of the nails, and place my hand into his side, I will never believe." Eight days later, his disciples were inside again, and Thomas was with them. Although the doors were locked, Jesus came and stood among them and said, "Peace be with you." Then he said to Thomas, "Put your finger here, and see my hands; and put out your hand, and place it in my side. Do not disbelieve, but believe." Thomas answered him, "My Lord and my God!" Jesus said to him, "Have you believed because you have seen me? Blessed are those who have not seen and yet have believed."

Biblical Narration

Poor Thomas!

What he expected with trepidation on the journey to Jerusalem has come to pass. The Master has been killed, and he and the other *disciples* have retreated in *fear* for their own lives. For his part, Thomas withdraws also from the company of his fellow followers, who remain *locked* behind closed doors.

In separating himself from the others, Thomas misses out on the opportunity to see his Lord alive again and in their midst. Locked behind the logic of his own thinking, he cannot, will not, believe it possible. Not even the *glad* tidings of his compatriots can shake him from his doldrums; in fact, their joy may make him feel even worse for *not* having been *with them* when the Lord returned. As a result, he remains obstinate and on his own. He wants, he needs, to see for himself. Otherwise, he will *never believe* it.

The Master obliges, but not until *eight days later*. Repeating the scene that the other apostles experienced and to which they testified, Jesus manifests Himself directly *to Thomas*. But unlike the first appearance, this time Jesus challenges His close companion, calling him out by name to make it real. He beckons the doubting disciple to go beyond his visual sense and grasp tactilely the truth of the Resurrection. Somehow knowing what Thomas had thought and said, the Master invites him to reach into His *side*, into the pierced flesh from which His Heart had poured out blood and water. Offering him that possibility, Jesus bids him to *believe*.

Thomas does. With or without actually touching the wounds of Jesus—the story does not say—Thomas undergoes a radical change of perspective. *Seeing Jesus* alive, he becomes a man of faith. He who had adamantly professed that he would never believe without tangible proof now confesses the belief that Jesus is his *Lord and God*. With that conversion of his own mind and heart, prompted by his visionary experience of the wounds that revealed the Sacred Heart, Thomas rejoins the other apostles as primary witnesses to the Resurrection.

From their testimony, the Christian tradition is born. The witness of those who actually saw the Risen Lord gives rise to the joyous announcement of the good news of salvation and, in turn, becomes the source of beatitude for all those in future ages *who have not seen, yet have believed*.

"Believing Is Seeing"

In this post-Resurrection account, the fourth Gospel narrates in straightforward fashion the change from incredulity to belief in the person of "doubting Thomas" and, by extension, the genesis of Easter faith in every Christian. That personal transformation hinges not merely on what the apostles see, but on how they see, a distinction that comes through more clearly in the Greek text of the story, which employs different terms in positing the connection between seeing and believing.

The "seeing" (from εἴδω) of the disciples gathered on that *first day of the week* was, at first, merely physical. Looking upon Jesus standing before them, they "see" (v. 20) with their eyes. They notice His hands and His side as He shows Himself to them. They sense that it really is Him, the One who was crucified. This is what Thomas also demands to "see" (v. 23). Later, Jesus invites him to do just that (v. 27).

But physical sight does not suffice. Appreciating the mystery, and coming to the fullness of faith, requires more than sense awareness. Through an experience of grace, the apostles come to a more profound perception of what it means to "have seen the Lord." They learn to "*see*" (from ὁράω) with the discerning eyes of their hearts. Attentive to the totality of their experience, they bear witness to Him whom they have beheld (v. 25). This, too, Thomas experiences in the presence of his wounded yet living Lord and God (v. 29).

The phenomenon of Christian spirituality builds on this vision, on this transformation of the believer into a person of faith. Like the Thomas who stood apart from the community of disciples, those closed in on their own wants and needs may think that "seeing is believing." But like the Thomas standing in the presence of the living Jesus, those open to an experience of the Sacred Heart realize that, in fact, "believing is seeing."

Salesian Spirituality

As a Doctor of the Church, St. Francis de Sales often speaks of faith, exploring its features as a revealed gift and as a developed virtue. As a master of spirituality, however, he looks to faith as a matter of the heart more so than of the mind.

He develops this perspective when he preaches about what almost led Thomas astray. In a sermon for the Sunday after Easter in 1620

(*Oeuvres*, 9:308-314), the saint pictures the incredulity of the apostle in terms analogous to "libertine persons who wish to have no other laws than those which their own will dictates to them." Basing his analysis on the thoughts of the Church Fathers, he examines three sources of this incredulity, all of which reside in the heart. The first is chagrin, that "sadness and ennui" which "obfuscates and troubles judgment" and endangers the soul by rejecting "correction and instruction and, in brief, all that is contrary to its own erroneous opinion." The second is jealousy and vanity, by which a person seeks for himself or herself what others enjoy, believes his or her own judgment to be proper, and becomes so opinionated as not to submit to the authority that others have. The third is the despair that derives from the preceding chagrin and jealousy; it leads Thomas to set conditions on his Master's appearance and to remain obstinate in demanding that the Lord show Himself as this lone apostle wanted.

Drawing a similar picture of Thomas's contrariness in a sermon on the apostle's feast day in 1622 (*Oeuvres*, 10:406-411), St. Francis de Sales exhorts his listeners to a greater fidelity. Wisely noting that we do not climb to complete perfection in one jump, but little by little (and by degrees), the saintly preacher reminds us that "it is necessary to have humility in order to receive that ray of divine light which is a purely gratuitous gift." He points out how "Our Lord, by his ineffable mercy, comes a second time just for St. Thomas" and "gives him in this way some proofs of the gentleness with which he treats sinners." Believing that the apostle did as the Lord invited him to do, St. Francis de Sales suggests that in that moment Thomas

> sensed a great divine warmth, principally when he put his hand into that precious space of the treasures of Divinity, when he touched that sacred heart so ardent with love. Being so astonished, he exclaimed "O my Lord and my God"

and was, at the same time, changed and rendered faithful, such that he has been a preacher of that faith like the other Apostles, and after having nobly worked for it, in the end he died for that same faith.

This Gospel narrative of Thomas's encounter with the Sacred Heart of the Risen Lord shows the affinity between divine love and human faith. For the apostle, the connection happens through physical contact; for we who meditate on this scene, it happens spiritually. As St. Francis de Sales explains in his *Treatise on the Love of God*:

> When God gives us faith, he enters into our soul and speaks to our mind. He does this not by way of discussion but by way of inspiration. So pleasantly does he propose to the intellect what it must believe that the will thereby receives such great complacence that it incites the intellect to consent to the truth and acquiesce in it without any doubt or opposition whatsoever.

By this loving encounter in the mind and heart, our lives are transformed, just as Thomas's was. In the end, says St. Francis de Sales, "this assurance which human reason finds in revealed things and the mysteries of faith begins in a loving sentiment of complacence that the will takes from the beauty and sweetness of the truth that has been proposed. Hence faith includes a first start of love which the heart feels for the things of God" (*Treatise*, 2:14).

Prayerful Inspiration

We who believe in the Resurrection can feel that loving complacence of God when we meditate upon the mystery of the Sacred Heart of Jesus. Encountering the Risen Lord through prayer, we can experience the same warmth of love and the same conviction of faith as did Thomas, whose apostolic witness assures us that the Heart of Jesus is, and will always be, alive and well.

Considerations

1. Reflect upon the state of the world with regard to religious faith, especially the indifference, or even antipathy, shown to Christianity. Ponder why the "nones" (those claiming no religious affiliation) are on the rise, especially among disaffected Catholics. Consider how the world is impacted by the dearth of witnesses to the Faith in the decreasing number of vocations to the priesthood and consecrated life. Picture the future of the Church with so many young people ignorant of, or resistant to, religious belief.

2. Examine yourself with regard to how you see your faith. To what extent do you approach it as a matter of the mind and depend on seeing proofs or evidence before you believe? Are you, at times, obstinate in your own religious opinions, especially if these are contrary to the teaching of the Church? How often do you open your heart to the presence of God before you in nature, other people, the sacraments, and so on?

3. Look into your own soul with regard to the mysteries of the Faith. Consider what inspirations you have already been blessed to receive. Wonder about the astonishing things of God that you have witnessed. Ponder anew what it means to say that Jesus is your Lord and your God.

Affections

1. Stir your heart to an appreciation for the gift of faith in the Risen Lord Jesus. Be thankful for all those who have witnessed that faith and passed it along to you. Regret those

times that you have turned away from bearing witness to that faith, or publicly criticized the truth of it, or impugned the good will of those who share it.

2. Humble yourself before the Lord standing in front of you as He stood before Thomas. Cast away any doubts you may have or demands you might make regarding God's presence. Open your heart to hope instead of despair by hearing Jesus say also to you, "Do not disbelieve, but believe."

3. Be astonished at how the Risen Lord continues to come back to you with proof of His mercy and love. Arouse in your heart the desire to be a person of faith and to share that faith with others.

Salesian Devotion

If for Thomas seeing was believing, then for us at prayer believing is seeing. From the gentle "touch" of God's love by way of revelation and inspiration come the assurance and certitude that our lives are forever changed. Based on this profound spiritual perception of the living Sacred Heart of Jesus, we seek to live a devout life that witnesses to our faith in the Resurrection.

Resolutions

1. On a *personal* level, what might you do to deepen your own faith? Perhaps you might devote more time to meditative prayer. Or you could learn more about the apostles, Church Fathers, or other saints who have historically witnessed to the Faith. Or you might simply make an extended retreat to enter more deeply into the new life of the Sacred Heart.

2. On a *relational* level, what might you do to give witness to the Risen Lord Jesus? Perhaps you might seek ways to speak

about the Faith through participation in parish organizations. Or you could volunteer to assist with programs of youth or adult faith formation. Or you might simply be more intentional about sharing the joy of your Lord and God in the ways that you encounter others.

3. On a *societal* level, what might you do to proclaim the good news of Christianity? Perhaps you might explore opportunities to participate in diocesan activities for the new evangelization. Or you could use your social media to promote the Faith in a spirit of reasonableness and charity. Or you might support reputable organizations in their work of communicating the truth of the gospel.

Recollections

1. In adoration before the Lord, give thanks for the ways in which the Risen Jesus has shown His Sacred Heart to you, and confess to Him again that He remains your Lord and your God.

2. Remember the inspirations you received in this meditation by calling to mind the image of Thomas *seeing* the living Jesus standing before him and receiving from Him the invitation to touch and be touched by the Sacred Heart.

3. Recall throughout the day this Salesian maxim: "We must neither ask anything nor refuse anything, but leave ourselves absolutely in the arms of divine Providence, without busying ourselves with any desires, except to will what God wills of us" (*Spiritual Conferences*, 400).

Conclusion

⊹

THE SACRED HEART OF JESUS
AS THE "SCHOOL OF LOVE"

The tradition of Salesian spirituality, in which St. Margaret Mary figures prominently, offers a view of life both optimistic and real. The dominant metaphor in this vision pictures a world of interconnected hearts—human and divine—to express the harmonious state of life and love to which human beings are eternally destined. But, as is clear from human history, we have not yet arrived there; in fact, as our own experience demonstrates, we have a long way to go.

Still, our journey to eternal life has begun and has been set on the right course thanks to God's "visitation" of this world in the person of His Son, Jesus. In His life, death, Resurrection, and Ascension, we discover all that we need for our eternal salvation. Particularly in His Passion on Calvary, where His Sacred Heart is pierced open to pour out the full graces of redemption, we find what St. Francis de Sales describes as a "school of love" for Christian wisdom.

Prayerfully incorporating his motto for the devout life,[84] the saint concludes his masterful *Treatise on the Love of God* with this mystical summary of the devout life:

> O love eternal, my soul needs and chooses you eternally! Ah, come Holy Spirit, and inflame our hearts with your love! To love—or to die! To die—and to love! To die to all other love in order to live in Jesus' love, so that we may not die eternally. But that we may live in your eternal love, O Savior of our souls, we eternally sing, "Live, Jesus! Jesus, I love! Live, Jesus whom I love! Jesus I love, Jesus who lives and reigns forever and ever. Amen." (*Treatise*, 12:13)

That mysticism comes to full display in devotion to the Sacred Heart of Jesus. Born of the visionary experiences of St. Margaret Mary Alacoque, the devotion enables us to comprehend the love of Christ for humanity by looking upon that sacred image and icon.

Jesus Himself tells us as much—in the only Gospel reference in which He describes the makeup of His Heart to us: "Come to me, all who labor and are heavy laden, and I will give you rest. Take my yoke upon you, and learn from me, for I am gentle and lowly in heart, and you will find rest for your souls. For my yoke is easy, and my burden is light" (Matt. 11:28-30).

Frequently cited in the corpus of St. Francis de Sales's writings, this alluring invitation serves as the cornerstone to the edifice of Salesian spirituality. As Wendy Wright explains:

---

[84] The saint used to write the expression "*Vive Jesus*" (abbreviated "V+J") on the top of the pages of his notes.

The invitation to learn from, to imitate, to follow, to be as Jesus receives the stress. And what is Jesus like? He is gentle and humble of heart. That is, the core of his being, his most essential self, the point from which all actions and thoughts flow—the heart—has the qualities of gentleness and humility. For Francis this was a radically countercultural idea, for most hearts are not gentle and humble but proud, grasping, and envious.... For him, this truth had eschatological significance, for Jesus the Christ came to overturn the standards of the world and enflesh a new standard of reality. Gentleness and humility were signs of the presence of the kingdom.[85]

Through meditative prayer, we tap into this new reality and respond to the divine plea by listening to what Jesus wishes to reveal to His own "little children." He says, "*Come to me*," to those who desire happiness—not to the self-proclaimed and self-serving followers of secular culture, whose perspectives are limited to this world. To those who seek meaning in life, He insists, "*Learn from me*"—rather than trusting in partial human knowledge and being guided by passions and inclinations, fickle as these will be. He can claim, "*I am gentle*," for His deeds show love and mercy shared with all the world, despite our indifference toward Him and our sins against Him. And He rightly identifies Himself as "lowly in *heart*," for He has need of nothing for Himself, but wants only for us to know how much we are loved and for us to return love for love by how we treat one another.

That love, which alone gives *rest for* our *souls*, comes from Him who revealed His Heart to St. Margaret Mary, "with all Its treasures

---

[85] Wendy Wright, *Francis de Sales: Introduction to the Devout Life and Treatise on the Love of God*, Crossroad Spiritual Legacy Series (New York: Crossroad, 1993), 78-79.

of love, mercy, grace, sanctification, and salvation. This He did," she writes, "in order that those who were willing to do all in their power to render and procure for Him honor, love, and glory might be enriched abundantly, even profusely, with these divine treasures of the Heart of God, which is their source."[86]

In this brief book of Salesian devotion, we have sought to unlock some of those treasures through a novena of meditations on the Sacred Heart of Jesus. Reading the Gospels, we find there narrative images sketched by the sacred authors that reveal

- a *pulsing* Heart, in which joy is manifest in the incarnate Child;
- a *beloved* Heart, which affirms the primacy of a filial relationship;
- a *compassionate* Heart, showing the divine response to human need;
- an *encouraging* Heart, which offers a remedy to fear;
- a *broken* Heart, wounded by love for all the world;
- an *abiding* Heart, making possible the endurance of divine love;
- a *troubled* Heart, in the passionate union of "pain in love and love in pain";
- a *pierced* Heart, sign of the price paid for our redemption;
- a *living* Heart, inviting faith in Him who is risen to new life.

Meditating upon these inspired images, we can comprehend the love of Christ by looking to His Sacred Heart. But each time we gaze prayerfully upon that icon of divine love, something else happens. Not only do we look upon it, but also it looks back at

---

[86] *Letters of St. Margaret Mary Alacoque*, 230.

us. If we allow it, this contemplative gaze will excite our minds, arouse our affections, and stir our wills to live a truly devout life. Gazing upon the Sacred Heart of Jesus draws us into a personal encounter with Him and invites us to dare to come close to love itself. Seeing that Heart of Christ, and being seen by it, helps us realize that our best hope in this world lies not in the fleeting emotions of our human hearts, but in the steadfast grace and power of the divine Heart. We can experience that saving grace and transforming power when we surrender our sins, our wounds, even our desires to Him who has opened His Heart for us with such indescribable mercy.

Centuries ago, in a secluded monastery in Paray-le-Monial, this treasure of divine love was opened to St. Margaret Mary Alacoque when the Lord Jesus appeared to her in prayer. There the Lord disclosed to her His Sacred Heart and instructed her to spread devotion to it throughout the world.

Now, more than a century after her canonization, we remain the beneficiaries of that Visitation nun's experience. May we, like her, never cease to "behold this Heart, which has so loved" the world.

+ May God Be Praised +

The Apostolic Pilgrimage of Pope John Paul II in France

(English translation of texts presented in Paray-le-Monial)
October 5, 1986

Letter to the Superior General of the Society of Jesus

To the Reverend Father Peter-Hans Kolvenbach,
Superior General of the Society of Jesus

In the course of my pilgrimage to Paray-le-Monial, I wished to come to pray in this chapel where the tomb of Blessed Claude de la Colombière is venerated. He was "the faithful servant" whom the Lord in His providential love gave as spiritual director to St. Margaret Mary Alacoque. Thus was he led, the first one, to disseminate His message. In a few years of religious life and intense ministry, he showed himself an "exemplary son" of the Society of Jesus to which, in the testimony of St. Margaret Mary herself, Christ had confided the task of spreading the cult of His divine Heart.

I know with what generosity the Society of Jesus has accepted this admirable mission and with what ardor it has sought to fulfill it as much as possible in the course of these last three centuries.

But I desire, on this solemn occasion, to exhort all the members of the Society to promote with still more zeal this devotion that corresponds more than ever to the expectations of our time.

In effect, if the Lord in His Providence had wanted that at the dawn of modern times, in the seventeenth century, a powerful impulse in favor of the devotion to the Heart of Christ should issue forth from Paray-le-Monial under the forms indicated in the revelations received by St. Margaret Mary, the essential elements of this devotion belong also in a permanent fashion to the spirituality of the Church throughout her history. For since the beginning, the Church has turned her gaze toward the Heart of Christ pierced on the Cross from which flowed blood and water, symbols of the sacraments that constitute the Church. And in the Heart of the incarnate Word, the Fathers of the Christian East and West have seen the beginning of the entire work of our salvation, fruit of the love of the divine Redeemer whose pierced Heart is a particularly expressive symbol.

The desire of "knowing intimately the Lord" and of "entering into conversation" with Him, heart to heart, is characteristic, thanks to the *Spiritual Exercises*, of the Ignatian spiritual dynamism and apostolate, entirely in service of the love of the Heart of God.

The Second Vatican Council, while reminding us that Christ, the incarnate Word, "has loved us with a human heart," assures us that "His message, far from diminishing man, serves his development by infusing light, life and freedom and, apart from Him, nothing can satisfy the human heart" (*Gaudium et Spes*, 21). From the Heart of Christ, the heart of man learns to know the true and unique sense of his life and his destiny, to comprehend the value of an authentic Christian life, to guard himself against certain perversions of the human heart, [and] to join filial love toward God to the love of the neighbor. Thus—and this is the true reparation requested by the Heart of the Savior—on the accumulated ruins of hate and violence will be built the civilization of [the love so desired, the reign of] the Heart of Christ.

For these reasons, I earnestly desire that you pursue with persevering action the dissemination of the true cult of the Heart of Christ, and that you be always ready to offer an efficacious assistance to my brothers in the episcopacy so as to promote this cult everywhere, by taking care to find the most adequate means to present it and to practice it, so that the man of today, with his own mentality and sensibility, discovers there the true response to his questions and his expectations.

In the same way as last year, on the occasion of the Congress of the Apostolate of Prayer, [when] I particularly confided to you this work strictly bound to the devotion to the Sacred Heart, today as well, in the course of my pilgrimage to Paray-le-Monial, I ask you to deploy every possible effort to accomplish always better the mission that Christ Himself has confided to you, the dissemination of the cult of His divine Heart.

The abundant spiritual fruits that devotion to the Heart of Jesus has produced are largely recognized. Expressed notably by the practice of the holy hour, of Confession, and of Communion on the first Fridays of the month, it has contributed to spurring generations of Christians to pray more and to participate more frequently in the Sacraments of Penance and of the Eucharist. These are desirable paths to propose to the faithful again today.

May the maternal protection of the Blessed Virgin Mary assist you. It was on her feast of the Visitation that this mission was confided to you in 1688. In your apostolic work, may it be for you support and comfort [to receive] the Apostolic Blessing that I give from the heart to the entire Society of Jesus, from Paray-le-Monial!

Behold This Heart

Discourse to the Monastery of the Visitation at Paray-le-Monial

"Behold this Heart which has so loved men that it has spared nothing but has utterly consumed and exhausted itself in order to show them its love."

With emotion, I would like to give thanks for this message received and transmitted here by St. Margaret Mary Alacoque. Near her tomb, I ask her to help people ceaselessly to discover the love of the Savior and to let themselves be penetrated by it.

Let us give thanks for the radiance of this monastery, remembering what Francis de Sales said to the Daughters of the Visitation: "They will have the Heart of Jesus, their crucified spouse, to dwell and rest there [while] in this world." I know that a myriad of nuns has been here, souls given to the Heart of Jesus.

Let us give thanks for the mystical experience of St. Margaret Mary. To her it was given, with a particular light but in a hidden existence, to know the power and the beauty of this love of Christ. In eucharistic adoration, she contemplated the Heart pierced for the salvation of the world, wounded for the sin of men, but also a "living source" as witnessed by the light that radiates from the wounds of His risen body.

Let us give thanks for the intimacy of the humble religious with the Savior. She generously offered suffering, which struck her in many forms, in union with the Passion of Christ, in reparation for the sin of the world. She recognized herself [to be] both a witness of the salvation worked by the Son of God and called to be associated [with it] by the offering of herself to the work of His mercy.

Let us give thanks for the privileged encounter of the holy religious with Blessed Claude de la Colombière. The support of this faithful disciple of St. Ignatius permitted Margaret Mary to overcome her doubts and to discern the authentic inspiration of her extraordinary experience. Their conversations are a model of equilibrium in spiritual counsel. Fr. de la Colombière, in great trials, himself received the illumined advice of her whom he counseled.

Let us give thanks for the vast development of eucharistic adoration and Holy Communion, which have taken from here a new impulse, [and] thanks to the worship of the Sacred Heart favored in particular by the Visitation and the Jesuit Fathers, approved in turn by the popes. The particular devotion of the first Fridays of the month has borne much fruit, thanks to the pressing messages received by Margaret Mary. And I cannot forget that the bishops of Poland had obtained from Clement XIII the Office and the Mass of the Sacred Heart nearly a century (1765) before the feast was extended to the universal Church (1856).

Let us give thanks for so many pastoral initiatives and religious foundations that found here a source of decisive inspiration.

With you who welcome me in this Chapel of Apparitions, the Sisters of the Visitation united to the other contemplative religious of the diocese, [and] with Bishop Gaidon and the chaplains of the sanctuary, let us invoke for all humanity, consecrated to the Sacred Heart by my predecessor Leo XIII, the inexhaustible grace of the redemptive love which flows from the Heart of Jesus.

Homily for the Mass Celebrated in Paray-le-Monial

1. *"I will give you a new heart"* (Ezek. *36:26*).

We find ourselves in a place where these words of the prophet Ezekiel resound with force. They have been confirmed here by a poor and hidden servant of the divine Heart of our Lord: St. Margaret Mary. Many times, in the course of history, the truth of this promise has been confirmed by revelation, in the Church, through the experience of saints, mystics, and souls consecrated to God. The entire history of Christian spirituality witnesses to it: the life of man (that of the heart) believing in God, pointed toward the future by hope, called to the communion of love—this life is that of the "interior" man. It is illumined by the admirable truth of the Heart of Jesus, who offers Himself for the world.

Why has the truth about the Heart of Jesus been confirmed here in a singular mode, in the seventeenth century, as on the threshold of modern times?

I am glad to meditate on this message in the land of Bourgogne, land of holiness, distinguished by [the abbeys of] Cîteaux and Cluny, where the gospel modeled the life and work of men.

I am glad to repeat the message of God rich in mercy in the diocese of Autun, which welcomes me. I cordially salute Bishop Armand le Bourgeois, Shepherd of this Church, and his auxiliary Bishop Maurice Gaidon. I salute the representatives of the civil authorities, both local and regional. I salute the entire people of God gathered here, the workers of the land and those of industry, the families, in particular the associations that animate their Christian life, the associations that love their Christian life, the seminarians who begin their journey toward the priesthood, the pilgrims of the Sacred Heart, especially the Emmanuel Community so closely attached to this place, as well as all those who come here to affirm their faith, their spirit of prayer, and their sense of the Church, in summer sessions or in other community initiatives. And I would like also to be near all those persons who, thanks to television, are following this celebration in their homes.

2. "I will give you a heart." God tells us this by way of the prophet. And the sense is clarified by the context. "I will pour out on you a pure water, and you will be purified" (Ezek. 36:25, my translation). Yes, God purifies the human heart. The heart, created to be the home of love, has become the central home of the rejection of God, of the sin of man who turns from God to attach himself to all sorts of "idols." It is then that the heart is "impure." But when the same interior place is opened to God, it finds again the "purity" of the image and likeness imprinted in him by the Creator from the beginning.

The heart is also the central home for the conversion that God desires from man and for man, in order to enter into His intimacy, into His love. God has created man in order that he be neither indifferent nor cold, but open to God. How beautiful are the words of the prophet: "I will take from you your heart of stone, and I will give you a heart of flesh" (Ezek. 36:26, my translation)! The heart of flesh, a heart that has a human sensibility and a heart capable of letting itself be seized by the breath of the Holy Spirit. It is then that Ezekiel says: "I will give you a new heart, I will place in you a new spirit … my spirit" (Ezek. 36:26–27, my translation).

Brothers and sisters, may each of us allow himself or herself to be purified and converted by the Spirit of the Lord! May each of us find in Him an inspiration for his or her life, a light for his or her future, a clarity to purify his or her desires!

Today, I would like to announce particularly to families the good news of an admirable gift: God gives the purity of heart; God permits [us] to live in true love!

3. The words of the prophet prefigure the profundity of the gospel experience. The salvation to come is already present.

But how will the Spirit come into the hearts of men? What will be the transformation so desired by God for Israel?

It will be the work of Jesus Christ: the eternal Son that God has not spared, but that He has given for all of us, in order to give us every grace with Him (cf. Rom. 8:32), in order to offer us everything with Him!

It will be the marvelous work of Jesus. For it to be revealed, it was necessary to wait until the end, until His death on the Cross. And when Christ "has delivered" His spirit into the hands of the Father (cf. Luke 23:46), then this event happens: "Then the soldiers came.... They came to Jesus and seeing that he was already dead ... one of the soldiers with his lance pierced his side, and immediately blood and water flowed out" (John 19:32–34, my translation).

The event appears "ordinary." On Golgotha, it is the last gesture in a Roman execution: the determination of the death of the condemned. Yes, He is dead, He is really dead!

And in His death, He reveals Himself until the end. The pierced Heart is His ultimate witness. John, the apostle who remained at the foot of the Cross, understood it; over the course of centuries, the disciples of Christ and the teachers of the Faith have understood it. In the seventeenth century, a religious of the Visitation received anew this witness at Paray-le-Monial; Margaret Mary transmitted it to the entire Church on the threshold of modern times.

By the Heart of His Son, pierced on the Cross, the Father has given us everything gratuitously. The Church and the world receive the Consoler: the Holy Spirit. Jesus had said: "When I depart, I will send him to you" (John 16:7, my translation). His Heart transpierced testifies that He "is departed." He sends now the Spirit of truth. The water which flows from His pierced side is the sign of the Holy Spirit: Jesus had announced to Nicodemus the new birth "by water and the Spirit." The words of the prophet are fulfilled: "I will give you a new heart, I will put into you a new spirit" (Ezek. 36:26, my translation).

4. St. Margaret Mary knew this admirable mystery, the overwhelming mystery of divine love. She knew completely the profundity of the words of Ezekiel: "I will give you a heart."

Throughout her hidden life in Christ, she was marked by the gift of this Heart that offers itself without limit to all human hearts. She was seized entirely by this divine mystery, as the admirable prayer of today's responsorial psalm expresses: "Bless the Lord, O my soul, all my being, bless his holy name!" (Psalm 103:1, my translation).

"All my being," meaning "all my heart"! Bless the Lord! ... Never forget any of His benefits. He pardons. He "heals." He "reclaims your life from the tomb." He "crowns you with love and tenderness." He is good and full of love. Slow to anger. Full of love: of merciful love, He who remembers "that we are stones" (Psalm 103:1–4, 14, my translation).

Him. Truly Him, the Christ.

5. All her life, St. Margaret Mary burned with the living flame of this love that Christ has come to ignite in the history of man.

Here, in this place of Paray-le-Monial, as once [did] the apostle Paul, the humble servant of God seemed to cry out to the entire world: "Who will be able to separate us from the love of Christ?"

Paul addressed himself to the first generation of Christians. They knew what "distress, anxiety, persecution, hunger and even nakedness" were [in the arenas, within the teeth of beasts]; they knew what danger and the sword were!

In the seventeenth century, the same question resounds, posed by Margaret Mary to Christians then, in Paray-le-Monial. In our time, the same question resounds, addressed to each of us. To each one in particular, when he or she considers his or her experience of family life.

Who breaks the bonds of love? Who extinguishes the love that enflames the homes?

6. We know it—the families in this time know trial and separation too often. Too many couples are poorly prepared for marriage. Too many couples are separated and know not how to keep the fidelity [they] promised, to accept the other such as he or she is, to love him or her despite his or her limits and weakness. Too many children are deprived of the stable support that they should find in the complementary harmony of their parents. And [there are] also some contradictions to the human truth of love, when one refuses to give life in a responsible manner, and when one reaches the point of causing an infant already conceived to die!

These are signs of a true malady that attacks persons, couples, children, [and] society itself!

The economic conditions, the influences of society, [and] the uncertainties of the future are invoked to explain the changes in the institution of the family. These weigh heavily, for sure, and it is necessary to remedy them. But that cannot justify renouncing a fundamental good, that of a stable unity of the family in the free and beautiful responsibility of those who pledge their love with the support of the indefatigable fidelity of the Creator and the Savior.

Has love not been too often reduced to the vertigo of individual desire or to the precariousness of feelings? By doing this, has it not been distanced from the true goodness which is found in the gift of self without reserve and in that which the Council calls "the noble ministry of life"? Is it not necessary to say clearly that to search for oneself by way of egoism more than to seek the good of the other, that is called sin? And that is to offend the Creator, source of all love, and Christ the Savior who has offered His wounded Heart in order that His brothers find again their vocation as beings who freely engage their love.

Yes, the essential question is always the same. The danger is always the same: that man be separated from love!

Man uprooted from the most profound terrain of his spiritual existence. Man condemned to have again a "heart of stone." Deprived of the "heart of flesh" that is capable of acting again justly [with regard] to good and evil. The heart sensible to the truth of man and to the truth of God. The heart capable of welcoming the breath of the Holy Spirit. The heart rendered strong by the power of God.

The essential problems of man—yesterday, today, and tomorrow—are situated at this level. The one who says, "I will give you a heart," comes to put into this word ("heart") everything by which man "becomes more."

7. The witness of many families shows well that the virtues of fidelity render [them] happy, that generosity of spouses for each other and together toward their children is a true source of goodness. The effort of self-mastery, the overcoming of the limits of each one, the perseverance in diverse moments of existence—all that leads to a fulfillment for which one can give thanks. Then it becomes possible to bear the trial that happens, to know [how] to pardon an offense, to welcome a child who suffers, to illuminate the life of the other, even weak or diminished, with the beauty of love.

Therefore, I would like to ask the shepherds and the animators who aid families to orient themselves to present clearly the positive support that constitutes for them the moral teaching of the Church. In today's confusing and contradictory situation, it is necessary to take up again the analysis and rules of life that have been set forth particularly in the Apostolic Exhortation *Familiaris Consortio*, following the synod of bishops, in expressing the whole of the doctrine of the Council and of the pontifical Magisterium. Vatican Council II recalled that "the divine law manifests the full meaning of conjugal love, it protects it and leads it to its truly human fulfillment" (*Gaudium et Spes*, 50).

8. Yes, thanks to the Sacrament of Marriage, in the covenant with divine wisdom, in the covenant with the infinite love of the Heart of Christ, families, it is given to you to develop in each of your members the richness of the human person, his or her vocation to the love of God and of men.

Know how to welcome the presence of the Heart of Christ by entrusting your home to Him. May He inspire your generosity, your fidelity to the sacrament where your covenant has been sealed before God. And may the charity of Christ help you to welcome and assist your brothers and sisters wounded by separations [and] left alone; your fraternal witness will make them better discover that the Lord does not cease to love those who suffer.

Animated by the Faith that has been transmitted to you, know how to awaken your children to the message of the gospel and to their role as artisans of justice and peace. Make them enter actively into the life of the Church. Do not pass them on to others, [but] cooperate with the shepherds and other educators in faith formation [and] in works of fraternal solidarity, the animation of the community. In your home life, openly give the Lord His place; pray together. Be faithful to listening to the Word of God, to the sacraments, and above all to Communion in the body of Christ given up for us. Participate regularly in Sunday Mass; it is the necessary gathering of Christians in church. There, you give thanks for your conjugal love bound "to the charity of Christ giving Himself on the Cross" (cf. *Familiaris Consortio*, 13). [There] you offer also your pains along with His saving sacrifice; each one, conscious of being a sinner, intercedes also for those of his or her brothers who, in many ways, distance themselves from their vocation and renounce accomplishing the will of the Father's love. [There] you receive from His mercy the purification and strength to pardon yourselves; you affirm your hope; you signal your fraternal communion by founding it on eucharistic Communion.

9. With Paul of Tarsus, with Margaret Mary, we proclaim the same certitude: neither death nor life, neither the present nor the future, neither the powers, nor any other creature, nothing will be able to separate us from the love of God that is in Jesus Christ. I am certain of it … nothing will ever be able to … !

Today, we find ourselves in this place of Paray-le-Monial to renew in ourselves this certitude: "I will give you a heart." Before the open Heart of Christ, let us seek to draw from it the true love that families need. The family cell is fundamental to build the civilization of love.

Everywhere—in society, in our villages, in our quarters, in our factories and our businesses, in our encounters between people and races—the "heart of stone," the dried-up heart, must be changed into [a] "heart of flesh," open to others, open to God. Peace demands it. The survival of humanity demands it. This goes beyond our strength. It is a gift of God. A gift of His love.

We have the certitude of His love!

APPENDIX 2
Devotional Prayers

✠

St. Margaret Mary's Act of Consecration to the Sacred Heart of Jesus[87]

O Sacred Heart of Jesus, I give and consecrate to Thee, my actions and pains, my sufferings and my life, in order that my entire being may be devoted to honor, love and glorify Thy Sacred Heart. It is my sincere determination to be and to do all for Thy love.

I renounce with all my heart, all that may be displeasing to Thee. I choose Thee, O Sacred Heart, for the only object of my love, the protector of my life, the pledge of my salvation, the remedy of my weakness and inconstancy, the repairer of my past defects, and my safe asylum at the hour of death.

Be then, O Heart of Goodness, my advocate near God the Father and save me from His just anger. O Heart of Love, in Thee I place all my confidence; I fear much from my own malice and weakness, but I hope all from Thy goodness. Destroy in me all that displeases or resists Thee.

Let Thy pure love be so deeply impressed on my heart that I may never forget or be separated from Thee. O Jesus, I implore

---

[87] The wording of the Act of Consecration is taken from https://vistyr.
org/prayers-devotions.

Thee, by Thy goodness, to let my name be written in Thy Sacred Heart, that living and dying in quality of Thy slave, I may find all my glory and happiness in Thee. Amen.

Litany to the Sacred Heart of Jesus[88]

In 1899 Pope Leo XIII approved this Litany of the Sacred Heart of Jesus for public use. This litany is actually a synthesis of several other litanies dating back to the seventeenth century. Father Croiset composed a litany in 1691 from which seventeen invocations were used by Venerable Anne Madeleine Remuzat when she composed her litany in 1718 at Marseille. She joined an additional ten invocations to those of Father Croiset, for a total of twenty-seven invocations. Six more invocations written by Sister Madeleine Joly of Dijon in 1686 were added by the Sacred Congregation for Rites when it was approved for public use in 1899. This makes a total of thirty-three invocations, one for each year of life of our Lord Jesus Christ. A partial indulgence is attached to this litany.

Invocation	Response
Lord, have mercy.	Lord, have mercy.
Christ, have mercy.	Christ, have mercy.
Lord, have mercy.	Lord, have mercy.
Christ, hear us.	Christ, hear us.
Christ, graciously hear us.	Christ, graciously hear us.
God the Father of Heaven,	have mercy on us.

---

[88] The wording of the litany, along with its explanation, is taken from www.ewtn.com/catholicism/teachings/litany-to-the-sacred-heart-of-jesus-270.

God the Son, Redeemer of the world,	have mercy on us.
God, the Holy Spirit,	have mercy on us.
Holy Trinity, One God,	have mercy on us.
Heart of Jesus, Son of the Eternal Father,	have mercy on us.
Heart of Jesus, formed by the Holy Spirit in the womb of the Virgin Mother,	have mercy on us.
Heart of Jesus, substantially united to the Word of God,	have mercy on us.
Heart of Jesus, of Infinite Majesty,	have mercy on us.
Heart of Jesus, Sacred Temple of God,	have mercy on us.
Heart of Jesus, Tabernacle of the Most High,	have mercy on us.
Heart of Jesus, House of God and Gate of Heaven,	have mercy on us.
Heart of Jesus, burning furnace of charity,	have mercy on us.
Heart of Jesus, abode of justice and love,	have mercy on us.
Heart of Jesus, full of goodness and love,	have mercy on us.
Heart of Jesus, abyss of all virtues,	have mercy on us.

Behold This Heart

Heart of Jesus, most worthy of all praise,	have mercy on us.
Heart of Jesus, king and center of all hearts,	have mercy on us.
Heart of Jesus, in whom are all treasures of wisdom and knowledge,	have mercy on us.
Heart of Jesus, in whom dwells the fullness of divinity,	have mercy on us.
Heart of Jesus, in whom the Father was well pleased,	have mercy on us.
Heart of Jesus, of whose fullness we have all received,	have mercy on us.
Heart of Jesus, desire of the everlasting hills,	have mercy on us.
Heart of Jesus, patient and most merciful,	have mercy on us.
Heart of Jesus, enriching all who invoke You,	have mercy on us.
Heart of Jesus, fountain of life and holiness,	have mercy on us.
Heart of Jesus, propitiation for our sins,	have mercy on us.
Heart of Jesus, loaded down with opprobrium,	have mercy on us.
Heart of Jesus, bruised for our offenses,	have mercy on us.

Heart of Jesus, obedient to death,	have mercy on us.
Heart of Jesus, pierced with a lance,	have mercy on us.
Heart of Jesus, source of all consolation,	have mercy on us.
Heart of Jesus, our life and resurrection,	have mercy on us.
Heart of Jesus, our peace and our reconciliation,	have mercy on us.
Heart of Jesus, victim for our sins,	have mercy on us.
Heart of Jesus, salvation of those who trust in You,	have mercy on us.
Heart of Jesus, hope of those who die in You,	have mercy on us.
Heart of Jesus, delight of all the Saints,	have mercy on us.
Lamb of God, who takes away the sins of the world,	spare us, O Lord.
Lamb of God, who takes away the sins of the world,	graciously hear us, O Lord.
Lamb of God, who takes away the sins of the world,	have mercy on us, O Lord.
Jesus, meek and humble of heart,	make our hearts like Yours.

Behold This Heart

Let us pray:

Almighty and eternal God, look upon the Heart of Your most beloved Son and upon the praises and satisfaction which He offers You in the name of sinners; and to those who implore Your mercy, in Your great goodness, grant forgiveness in the name of the same Jesus Christ, Your Son, who lives and reigns with You forever and ever. Amen.

Chaplet of the Sacred Heart[89]

The small beads represent the thirty-three years of the mortal life of our Lord. The first thirty recall to mind the years of His private life and are divided into five groups of six; the three on the pendant recall the public life of the Savior.

After the Sign of the Cross:

> Soul of Christ, sanctify me.
> Body of Christ, save me.
> Blood of Christ, inebriate me.
> Water from Christ's side, wash me.
> Passion of Christ, strengthen me.
> O good Jesus, hear me.
> Within Thy wounds hide me.
> Suffer me not to be separated from Thee.
> From the malicious enemy defend me.
> In the hour of my death call me.
> And bid me come unto Thee,
> That I may praise Thee with Thy saints

---

[89] The wording of the chaplet, along with its explanation, is taken from https://vistyr.org/prayers-devotions.

and with Thy angels
Forever and ever. Amen.

On each large bead:

Jesus, meek and humble of heart, make my heart like unto
Thine.

On each small bead:

Sweet Heart of Jesus, be Thou my love!

At the end of each group of six:

Sweet Heart of Mary, be my salvation!

On the final three small beads:

Sweet Heart of Jesus, be Thou my love!

On the Sacred Heart Badge to conclude:

Sacred Heart of Jesus, have mercy on us.
Immaculate Heart of Mary, pray for us.

May the Sacred Heart of Jesus be praised, glorified, loved,
and preserved throughout the world now and forever more.
Amen.

Novena to the Sacred Heart of Jesus[90]

O my Jesus, you have said: "Truly I say to you, ask and you will
receive, seek and you will find, knock and it will be opened to

---

[90] The wording of this novena is taken from www.thesacredheart.com/
shdnshj.htm.

you." Behold I knock, I seek and ask for the grace of ... (*here name your request*).

Our Father ... Hail Mary ... Glory Be to the Father ...
Sacred Heart of Jesus, I place all my trust in you.

O my Jesus, you have said: "Truly I say to you, if you ask anything of the Father in my name, he will give it to you." Behold, in your name, I ask the Father for the grace of ... (*here name your request*).

Our Father ... Hail Mary ... Glory Be to the Father ...
Sacred Heart of Jesus, I place all my trust in you.

O my Jesus, you have said: "Truly I say to you, heaven and earth will pass away but my words will not pass away." Encouraged by your infallible words I now ask for the grace of ... (*here name your request*).

Our Father ... Hail Mary ... Glory Be to the Father ...
Sacred Heart of Jesus, I place all my trust in you.

O Sacred Heart of Jesus, for whom it is impossible not to have compassion on the afflicted, have pity on us miserable sinners and grant us the grace which we ask of you, through the Sorrowful and Immaculate Heart of Mary, your tender Mother and ours.

Say the Hail, Holy Queen and add: "St. Joseph, foster father of Jesus, pray for us."

Novena Prayer of Confidence to the Sacred Heart of Jesus[91]

Lord Jesus!
To Your Sacred Heart I confide … (*intention*)
Only look …
Then do what Your Heart inspires …
Let Your Heart decide …
I count on It …
I trust in It …
I throw myself on Its Mercy …
Lord Jesus! You Will Not Fail Me!

Glory be to the Father and to the Son and to the Holy Spirit, as it was in the beginning, is now, and ever shall be, world without end. Amen. (three times)

St. Margaret Mary Alacoque, pray for me.

Guard of Honor[92]

Formed as an Association of the Faithful, the Guard of Honor of the Sacred Heart saw first light on March 13, 1863, at the Monastery of the Visitation of Holy Mary at Bourg-en-Bresse, France. To be a member, you must be properly registered at an official center (i.e., a Visitation Monastery).

---

[91] The wording of this Novena Prayer is taken from vistyr.org/prayers-devotions.

[92] This description is edited from information made available by the Visitation Monastery at Tyringham, which serves as the National Center for the Guard of Honor, USA. Related information can be found at www.guardofhonor-usa.org.

Behold This Heart

The Guard of Honor has its origins at Calvary, its foundation in the Wounded Heart of Jesus, its model in the first 'Guard of Honor': the Blessed Virgin Mary, St. John, and St. Mary Magdalene. They were the ones who stood by the abandoned Cross when the Heart of Christ was pierced by the lance.

* The main end of the Guard of Honor is to console the wounded Heart of Jesus by offering Him a threefold homage of glory, love and reparation.
* The Association aspires to ensure that at all hours of the day, fervent Christians are attentive to Christ's burning love for us.
* To this end, the members choose one hour of the day to be attentive to the presence of Jesus. It is not necessary to spend the Hour of Guard in prayer, nor in church. At their chosen hour, members, without changing any of their usual occupations, place themselves in spirit at the foot of the tabernacle. There they offer to Jesus their thoughts, words, actions, and sufferings, and above all their desire to console His divine Heart by their love.
* An additional *Hour of Mercy* may also be chosen for the intention of a special person or persons, family, or social group in the spirit of reparation. Because of the lack of faith and abandonment of the practice of religion of many—parents, spouses and friends have taken it upon themselves to offer an "Hour of Mercy" for the conversion of one or more of their loved ones.
* All members are highly recommended to participate in the First Friday Mass. Frequent sacramental communion is also highly recommended.

The Holy Hour[93]

Its History

In 1674, Jesus appeared to St. Margaret Mary Alacoque (1647– 1690) while she was in adoration. He spoke about Gethsemane and told her: "Here I suffered inwardly more than in the rest of my passion because I was totally alone, abandoned by heaven and earth, burdened with the sins of mankind. . . . In order for you to be united with me, in the humble prayer that I presented to my Father in the midst of all that anguish, you will arise between eleven o'clock and midnight, and prostrate yourself in adoration for one hour, with me." In that hour she participated in the sorrow of Jesus in Gethsemane. From this, the holy hour was born. It is based on three principal characteristics: prayer of reparation, union with the suffering Jesus in Gethsemane, and actions of humiliation.

How to Pray the Holy Hour

This is an hour of meditation on the agony of Jesus in the Garden of Gethsemane. One can do the holy hour by praying vocally or mentally, without any need to choose any particular type of prayer. The spirit that guides prayer is that of sharing with Jesus that moment: to suffer with Him, to live once again His anguish, His struggle, His battle, His resistance to that chalice of bitterness. But it also means living with Him true joy, that sentiment of peace that

---

[93] This explanation of the Holy Hour is excerpted from text found at https://www.horasancta.org/en/#ora-santa. Additional information, including a list of various prayers for "Holy Hours" can be found at www.usccb.org/prayer-and-worship/prayers-and-devotions/ eucharistic-devotion.

is born out of abandoning oneself to the will of the Father, being certain of His love for us.

Where to Pray the Holy Hour

One can pray during a holy hour in church, in the presence of the Holy Sacrament. If this is not possible, any place can be suitable for prayer. No circumstance or place can hinder our effort to enter into our hearts and remain with Him.

Promises of the Sacred Heart Given to Margaret Mary Alacoque[94]

1. I will give them all the graces necessary in their state of life.
2. I will give peace in their families and will unite families that are divided.
3. I will console them in all their troubles.
4. I will be their refuge during life and above all in death.
5. I will bestow the blessings of heaven on all their enterprises.
6. Sinners shall find in my Heart the source and infinite ocean of mercy.
7. Tepid souls shall become fervent.
8. Fervent souls shall rise quickly to great perfection.
9. I will bless those places wherein the image of my Heart shall be exposed and honored and will imprint my love on the hearts of those who would wear this image on their person. I will also destroy in them all disordered movements.
10. I will give to priests who are animated by a tender devotion to my divine Heart the gift of touching the most hardened hearts.
11. Those who promote this devotion shall have their names written in my Heart, never to be effaced.
12. I promise you in the excessive mercy of my Heart that my all-powerful love will grant to all those who communicate on the first Friday in nine consecutive months, the grace of final penitence: they will not die in my disgrace, nor without receiving their sacraments. My divine Heart shall be their safe refuge in this last moment.

---

[94] This text of the Promises is given in Wendy M. Wright, *Sacred Heart: Gateway to God* (Maryknoll, NY: Orbis Books, 2001), 127.

Bibliography

PRIMARY SOURCES
(authored by St. Francis de Sales or St. Jane de Chantal)

Introduction to the Devout Life. Translated with an introduction and notes by John K. Ryan. New York: Image Books, 1972.

Multiple English translations of this work exist. For this reason, in-text citations refer to this work by part:chapter(s). When quoted directly, the translation listed above is used.

Letters of Spiritual Direction. Classics of Western Spirituality. Translated by Péronne Marie Thibert, V.H.M. Selected and introduced by Wendy M. Wright and Joseph F. Power, O.S.F.S. Mahwah, NJ: Paulist Press, 1988.

Letters to Persons in Religion. Volume 4 of the Library of St. Francis de Sales. Translated by Very Rev. Canon Mackey, O.S.B. London: Burns and Oates, 1894.

Letters to Persons in the World. Volume 1 of the Library of St. Francis de Sales. Translated by Very Rev. Canon Mackey, O.S.B. London: Burns and Oates, n.d.

Oeuvres de Saint François de Sales: édition complète. 27 tomes. Annecy, France: Monastère de la Visitation, 1892–1964.

In-text citations refer to this work by tome:page(s). Unless otherwise noted, all translations are the author's.

On the Preacher and Preaching. Translated by John K. Ryan. Washington, DC: Henry Regnery, 1964.

Selected Letters. Translated with an introduction by Elisabeth Stopp. New York: Harper and Brothers, 1960.

The Sermons of St. Francis de Sales on Lent, Given in the Year 1622. Edited by Lewis S. Fiorelli, O.S.F.S. Translated by Nuns of the Visitation. Rockford, IL: TAN Books and Publishers, 1987.

The Sermons of St. Francis de Sales on Our Lady. Edited by Lewis S. Fiorelli, O.S.F.S. Translated by Nuns of the Visitation. Rockford, IL: TAN Books and Publishers, 1985.

The Spiritual Conferences. Translated by Abbot Gasquet and Canon Mackey, O.S.B. London: Burns Oates and Washbourne, 1923.

St. Francis de Sales: A Testimony by St. Chantal. Translated by Elisabeth Stopp. Hyattsville, MD: Institute of Salesian Studies, 1967.

Thy Will Be Done: Letters to Persons in the World. Manchester, NH: Sophia Institute Press, 1995.

Treatise on the Love of God. 2 vols. Translated with an introduction and notes by John K. Ryan. Rockford, IL: TAN Books and Publishers, 1975.

Multiple English translations of this work exist. For this reason, in-text citations refer to this work by book:chapter(s). When quoted directly, the translation listed above is used.

SALESIAN SPIRITUALITY
Abruzzese, John A. *The Theology of Hearts in the Writings of Saint Francis de Sales.* Rome: Pontifical University of St. Thomas Aquinas, 1983.

Chorpenning, Joseph. "The Dynamics of Divine Love: Francis de Sales's Picturing of the Biblical Mystery of the Visitation." In *Ut pictura amor: The Reflexive Imagery of Love in Artistic Theory and Practice, 1500–1700*. Edited by Walter S. Melion, Joanna Woodall, and Michael Zell. Leiden, Netherlands: Brill, 2017, 485–531.

——. "*Lectio Divina* and Francis de Sales's Picturing of the Interconnection of Divine and Human Hearts." In *Imago Exegetica: Visual Images as Exegetical Instruments, 1400–1700*. Edited by Walter S. Melion, James Clifton, and Michel Weemans. Leiden, Netherlands: Brill, 2014, 449–477.

——. "Pilgrimage with the Redeemer in the Womb: St. Francis de Sales's 1610 Meditation on the Biblical Mystery of the Visitation." In *In Nocte Consilium: Studies in Emblematics in Honor of Pedro F. Campa*. Edited by John T. Cull and Peter M. Daly. Baden-Baden, Germany: Verlag Valentin Koerner, 2011, 323–339.

Dailey, Thomas. *Live Today Well: St. Francis de Sales's Simple Approach to Holiness*. Manchester, NH: Sophia Institute Press, 2015.

——. "Playful Prayer: Imagination and the Task of Theology in a Salesian Perspective." In *Salesian Spirituality: Catalyst to Collaboration*. Edited by William Ruhl. Washington, DC: De Sales School of Theology, 1993, 169–188.

——. *Praying with Francis de Sales*. Companions for the Journey. Winona, MN: St. Mary's Press, 1997.

Ravier, André, S.J. *Francis de Sales: Sage and Saint*. Translated by Joseph Bowler, O.S.F.S. San Francisco: Ignatius Press, 1988.

Stopp, Elisabeth. *Hidden in God: Essays and Talks on St. Jane Frances de Chantal.* Edited by Terence O'Reilly. Philadelphia: St. Joseph's University Press, 1999.

Wright, Wendy. *Bond of Perfection: Jeanne de Chantal and François de Sales.* Mahwah, NJ: Paulist Press, 1983.

——. *Francis de Sales: Introduction to the Devout Life and Treatise on the Love of God.* Crossroad Spiritual Legacy Series. New York: Crossroad, 1993.

——. *Heart Speaks to Heart: The Salesian Tradition.* Traditions of Christian Spirituality Series. Maryknoll, NY: Orbis Books, 2004.

——. "'That Is What It Is Made For': The Image of the Heart in the Spirituality of Francis de Sales and Jane de Chantal." In *Spiritualities of the Heart: Approaches to Personal Wholeness in Christian Tradition.* Edited by Annice Callahan. Mahwah, NJ: Paulist Press, 1990, 143–158.

ST. MARGARET MARY ALACOQUE

The Autobiography of Saint Margaret Mary. Translation of the authentic French text (1930) by the Sisters of the Visitation. Rockford, IL: TAN Books and Publishers, 1986.

The Letters of St. Margaret Mary Alacoque. Translated from the French of the revised Gauthey edition of 1920 by Fr. Clarence H. Herbst, S.J. Rockford, IL: TAN Books and Publishers, 1997.

Bougaud, Rt. Rev. Émile. *The Life of Saint Margaret Mary Alacoque.* Translated by a Visitandine of Baltimore. Rockford, IL: TAN Books and Publishers, 1990.

Mattes, Anton. "Devotion to the Heart of Jesus in Modern Times: The Influence of Saint Margaret Mary Alacoque." In *Faith in Christ and the Worship of Christ: New Approaches to Devotion to Christ.* Edited by Leo Scheffczyk. Translated by Graham Harrison. San Francisco: Ignatius Press, 1986, 101–117.

Wright, Wendy. "Inside My Body Is the Body of God: Margaret Mary Alacoque and the Tradition of Embodied Mysticism." In *The Mystical Gesture: Essays on Medieval and Early Modern Spiritual Culture in Honor of Mary E. Giles.* Edited by Robert Boenig. Aldershot, UK: Ashgate, 2000, 185–192.

———. "Margaret Mary Alacoque and the Relational Mystery of the Visitation of Holy Mary." Online Journal, *Theological Review of the Episcopal Academy* (Spring 2006).

SACRED HEART

Ciappi, Mario Luigi. *Towards a Civilization of Love: A Symposium on the Scriptural and Theological Foundations of the Devotion to the Heart of Jesus.* San Francisco: Ignatius Press, 1985.

Costa, Anne. *Healing Promises: The Essential Guide to the Sacred Heart.* Cincinnati, OH: Franciscan Media, 2017.

Croiset, Rev. John. *The Devotion to the Sacred Heart of Jesus: How to Practice the Sacred Heart Devotion.* 2nd ed. Rockford, IL: TAN Books and Publishers, 2007.

Kubicki, James. *A Heart on Fire: Rediscovering Devotion to the Sacred Heart of Jesus.* Notre Dame, IN: Ave Maria Press, 2012.

McNamara, Martin. "A New Heart for a New World: A New Approach to Theology of Sacred Heart Devotion: Some

Biblical Evidence." *Irish Theological Quarterly* 56, no. 3 (1990): 201–228.

Morgan, David. "Rhetoric of the Heart: Figuring the Body in Devotion to the Sacred Heart." In *Things: Religion and the Question of Materiality.* Edited by Dick Houtman and Birgit Meyer. New York: Fordham University Press, 2012, 90–111.

———. *The Sacred Heart of Jesus: The Visual Evolution of a Devotion.* Amsterdam: Amsterdam University, 2008.

———. "The Visual Piety of the Sacred Heart." *Material Religion* 13, no. 2 (2017): 233–236.

O'Donnell, Timothy. *Heart of the Redeemer: An Apologia for the Contemporary and Perennial Value of the Devotion to the Sacred Heart of Jesus.* 2nd ed. San Francisco: Ignatius Press, 2017.

Quinlan, Michael. "History of Devotion to the Sacred Heart: St. Francis de Sales and the Visitation Nuns." *Irish Ecclesiastical Record*, 5th series, 60, no. 2 (August 1942): 102–112.

Richo, David. *The Sacred Heart of the World: Restoring Mystical Devotion to Our Spiritual Life.* Mahwah, NJ: Paulist Press, 2007.

Sisters of the Visitation of Holy Mary. *Stations of the Sacred Heart.* Stockbridge, MA: Marian Press, 2019.

Stierli, Joseph, ed. *Heart of the Saviour: A Symposium on Sacred Heart Devotion.* Translated by Paul Andrews. New York: Herder and Herder, 1958.

Weber, Jeanne. "Devotion to the Sacred Heart: History, Theology, and Liturgical Celebration." *Worship* 72, no. 3 (May 1998): 236–254.

Wright, Wendy. *Sacred Heart: Gateway to God*. Maryknoll, NY: Orbis Books, 2001.

———. "Transformed Seeing: Visual Devotional Imagery and the Shape of the Imagination—The Case of the Sacred Heart." *Studia Mystica* 22 (2001): 97–109.

———. "A Wide and Fleshy Love: Images, Imagination, and the Heart of God." *Studies in Spirituality* 10 (2000): 255–274.

Image Credits

✛

2. *The Sacred Heart*, engraving by A. Debrie, Wellcome Library.

12. Sacred Heart mosaic, Le Sanctuaire du Sacré-Coeur, Paray-le-Monial (2BN3EJT) © Godong / Alamy Stock Photo.

14. St. Francis de Sales portrait (RYKM60) © Godong / Alamy Stock Photo.

18. Jane Frances de Chantal portrait (RYKM60) © Godong / Alamy Stock Photo.

21. *San Francisco de Sales*, by Francisco Bayeu y Subías, eighteenth century, Museo del Prado, Madrid, Wikimedia Commons.

26. *St. Margaret Mary Alacoque*, used with permission of Sister Susan Marie, V.H.M.

29. *St. Margaret Mary Alacoque*, by Francesco Podesti (F55BA4) © colaimages / Alamy Stock Photo.

38. Albert Flamen (ca. 1620–after 1669), Emblem XXXI, in Adrien Gambart, *La vie symbolique du bienheureux François de Sales [...] comprise sous le voile de 52 emblèmes [...]* (Paris, 1664). Photo: courtesy Saint Joseph's University Press, Philadelphia.

42. St. Margaret Mary's depiction of the Sacred Heart of Jesus, uploaded by ADVENIAT REGNUM TUUM™, https://i.pinimg.com/originals/33/aa/97/33aa97b2243256ca84c97b3cd183cebf.jpg.

43. Sketches of the Profession Cross, Oblates of St. Francis de Sales, http://www.oblates.us/our-charism/cross-and-shield/.

44. Sacred Heart etching (Wellcome Images), Wikimedia Commons.

47. *Sacro cuore di Jesù,* by Pompeo Batoni, 1767, Chapel of Il Gesù, Rome, Wikimedia Commons https://commons.wikimedia.org/wiki/File:SacredHeartBatoni.jpg.

49. *The Sacred Heart,* by Lattanzio Querena, Church of Nome di Gesù, Venice, image courtesy of Didier Descouens, Wikimedia Commons.

60. *Sacred Heart of Jesus* (325142816), St. Nicholas Cathedral, Ljubljana, Slovenia © Zvonimir Atletic / Shutterstock.

64. *The Visitation,* by Gerónimo Antonio de Ezquerra, ca. 1737, Carmen Thyssen Museum, Wikimedia Commons.

74. *The Baptism of Christ,* by Antoine Coypel, ca. 1690, Los Angeles County Museum of Art, Wikimedia Commons.

84. *The Feeding of the Multitude,* by the Limbourg brothers, 1411–1416, Musée Condé, Wikimedia Commons.

94. *Jesus Walking on the Sea of Galilee,* by Paul Brill, 1590s, Museum of John Paul II Collection, Wikimedia Commons.

104. *Jesus Wept,* by James Tissot, 1886-1894, Brooklyn Museum, Wikimedia Commons.

114. Initial from choir book with Christ teaching the Twelve Apostles, early fifteenth century (R4X5T4), Italy © Album / Alamy Stock Photo.

124. *Christ in the Garden of Gethsemane,* by Lucas Cranach the Elder, ca. 1540, Museum Kunstpalast, Wikimedia Commons.

134. *Christ on the Cross between the Two Thieves,* by Peter Paul Rubens, 1619–1620, Royal Museum of Fine Arts, Antwerp, Wikimedia Commons.

146. *The Incredulity of Thomas,* by Maerten de Vos, 1574, Royal Museum of Fine Arts, Antwerp, Wikimedia Commons.

156. *La Santísima Trinidad*, by Corrado Giaquinto, 1754, Museo del Prado, Madrid.
162. Pope John Paul II, courtesy Rob Croes / Anefo, Wikimedia Commons.
176. *Sacred Heart of Jesus with Saint Ignatius of Loyola and Saint Louis Gonzaga*, by José de Páez, https://pbs.twimg.com/media/Dj dMlXtUwAANl2L?format=jpg&name=large.

About the Author

✟

Reverend Thomas F. Dailey, O.S.F.S., is a priest in the religious congregation of the Oblates of St. Francis de Sales. He holds the John Cardinal Foley Chair of Homiletics and Social Communications at Saint Charles Borromeo Seminary in the Archdiocese of Philadelphia and is a current member of the Academy of Catholic Theology. In the realm of Salesian studies, he has authored *Live Today Well* (Sophia Institute Press, 2015) and *Praying with Francis de Sales* (St. Mary's Press, 1997), contributed chapters to several academic books, written a dozen articles in pastoral journals, and published numerous commentaries for news agencies and websites. A member of the Catholic Speakers Organization, he frequently offers conferences and retreats based on Salesian spirituality.

Sophia Institute

Sophia Institute is a nonprofit institution that seeks to nurture the spiritual, moral, and cultural life of souls and to spread the Gospel of Christ in conformity with the authentic teachings of the Roman Catholic Church.

Sophia Institute Press fulfills this mission by offering translations, reprints, and new publications that afford readers a rich source of the enduring wisdom of mankind.

Sophia Institute also operates the popular online resource CatholicExchange.com. *Catholic Exchange* provides world news from a Catholic perspective as well as daily devotionals and articles that will help readers to grow in holiness and live a life consistent with the teachings of the Church.

In 2013, Sophia Institute launched Sophia Institute for Teachers to renew and rebuild Catholic culture through service to Catholic education. With the goal of nurturing the spiritual, moral, and cultural life of souls, and an abiding respect for the role and work of teachers, we strive to provide materials and programs that are at once enlightening to the mind and ennobling to the heart; faithful and complete, as well as useful and practical.

Sophia Institute gratefully recognizes the Solidarity Association for preserving and encouraging the growth of our apostolate over the course of many years. Without their generous and timely support, this book would not be in your hands.

www.SophiaInstitute.com
www.CatholicExchange.com
www.SophiaInstituteforTeachers.org

Sophia Institute Press® is a registered trademark of Sophia Institute.
Sophia Institute is a tax-exempt institution as defined by the
Internal Revenue Code, Section 501(c)(3). Tax ID 22-2548708.